Frances Burney

THE WORLD OF 'FEMALE DIFFICULTIES'

Frances Burney

THE WORLD OF 'FEMALE DIFFICULTIES'

Katharine M. Rogers

RESEARCH PROFESSOR
THE AMERICAN UNIVERSITY, WASHINGTON

HARVESTER WHEATSHEAF

New York   London   Toronto   Sydney   Tokyo   Singapore

First published 1990 by
Harvester Wheatsheaf
66 Wood Lane End, Hemel Hempstead
Hertfordshire HP2 4RG
A division of
Simon & Schuster International Group

Typeset in 10/13pt Palatino
by Keyboard Services, Luton, Beds

Printed and bound in Great Britain by
Billing and Sons Ltd, Worcester

British Library Cataloguing in Publication Data

Rogers, Katharine M. (Katharine Munzer), *1932–*
    Frances Burney: the world of 'Female Difficulties'
    1. Fiction in English. Burney, Fanny, 1752–1840
    I. Title
    823.6

ISBN 0-7108-1250-7

---

1 2 3 4 5   94 93 92 91 90

Contents

Introduction

WHEN JULIET, the heroine of Frances Burney's *The Wanderer, or Female Difficulties* (1814), saw the man she loved going to risk his life in Robespierre's France, she longed to run and stop him, and thereby 'to forfeit, by one dauntless stroke, the delicacy which, as yet, had, through life, been the prominent feature of her character.' But she restrained her impulse, for 'habits which have been formed upon principle, and embellished by self-approbation, withstand, upon the smallest reflection, every wish, and every feeling that would excite their violation.' She therefore confined herself to silent prayer (818). Perhaps it is unfair to quote these sentences, since resolution and independence are equally prominent features of Juliet's character, as Burney drew it; and *The Wanderer* as a whole presents a grimly realistic picture of this woman's struggles in a society that will not help her and does everything it can to disable her from helping herself.

Recent studies of Burney, notably Margaret Anne Doody's *Frances Burney: The Life in the Works* and Julia L. Epstein's *The Iron Pen: Frances Burney and the Politics of Women's Writing*, have rightly emphasized her complex understanding of women's genuine problems and her angry protest against the restrictions imposed by her society. Yet we cannot ignore Burney's conventional side. In part she accepted the same restrictive feminine morality she gave her heroine, so appropriately expressed in the fussy, stilted style of this passage. Avoiding indelicacy and avoiding criticism were issues of great importance to author as well as character. As an elderly woman, Burney defined her method of making moral decisions in these terms: 'the fear of doing Wrong has been always the leading principle of my internal guidance' (*The Journals and Letters of Fanny Burney*, hereafter referred to as *JL*, 10:878).[1]

Many episodes in Burney's life show her deference to conventional feminine ideals. She gave up a promising career as a playwright because her mentors aroused her fears that comic writing for the stage was indelicate. When Samuel Johnson asked her why he never saw her with a book in her hand, she replied that she dreaded being thought studious and affected (*Diary and Letters of Madame d'Arblay*, hereafter referred to as *DL* 1:135). She primly refused to discuss or even hear about politics, on the grounds that it was 'by no means a female business' (*DL* 3:495). She broke with her best friend, Hester Thrale, for making an unconventional love match after her first husband's death and thereby revealing unseemly passion. When her sister Susanna, the person closest to her in the world, desperately wished to separate from her tyrannical husband rather than accompany him to Ireland, Frances urged her to fulfill her wifely duties (*JL* 3:200, n.2). And she exacted the same standards of obedience from herself. She would have married a man she did not care for if her adored father had merely advised her to do so. To gratify him, she accepted a position at Court that she knew would deaden her mind and feelings; and when, after five awful years, he gave her permission to resign, she was filled with gratitude.

Even in the eighteenth-century context, Burney's subduing of self in the interests of feminine propriety was excessive. Other intelligent, articulate women of the period, equally committed to ladylike decorum and conservative politics, were less restricted. Elizabeth Carter declared she would do nothing without her father's consent. Nonetheless, she managed to lead her life as she wanted to – she never married and had no difficulty in refusing the inappropriate position at

Court that she was offered; she spent her time studying languages and eventually made herself a little fortune by translating Epictetus. Hannah More, at least as conservative as Burney in theory, did very much what she wanted to all her life and did not flinch from political action: not only in support of the Establishment, as she preached due submission to the lower orders, but in such subversive activities as teaching poor people to read and campaigning against the African slave trade.

On the other hand, there is ample evidence that Burney was a vital woman, capable of independent thinking and resistance to the restrictive conventions that she explicitly upheld. This appears most obviously in her creative achievement – the journals that brilliantly recreate her own experience and the four novels that present her view of woman's situation and problems. Writing, she recognized, was essential to her psychological survival. But it was not the only example of successful self-assertion. When she fell in love with a penniless French *émigré* and her father disapproved, she agonized – but she married Alexandre d'Arblay. And there are smaller examples of an intellectual vitality that could not be quenched. One time during her Court service, the royal family and their retainers toured Oxford. It was an exhausting day for the retainers, who had to stand for hours and got nothing to eat. Nevertheless, she was so interested by the buildings that she felt 'a consciousness to pleasure revived' in herself, 'which had long lain nearly dormant.' When at last they got to Trinity College Library and the Queen graciously allowed her ladies to be seated, everyone but Burney collapsed limply onto chairs. But she spent every minute of her time running around to look at the books, her interest making her oblivious to her fatigue (*DL* 2:462–72).

Burney's life, her journals and her novels express timidity, stultifying conventionality, self-suppressing submission to others' wishes and to her own narrow ideals of proper behaviour. And they constantly show vitality breaking through in the form of imaginative insight, of strength and resourcefulness, of laughter at pompous authority, of truth to feeling, of simple enjoyment and curiosity. The same woman who shrank from attending a school prize-giving ceremony without her husband sallied forth alone across a war zone, defying brutal Prussian commanders along the way, in order to be with him when he needed her (*JL* 6:554, 8:478–516). The woman who could see no flaw in her father or her queen skewered pompous authority in the form of the prosing cleric Dr King (*The Early Diary of Frances Burney 1768–1778*, hereafter referred to as *ED* 1:119, 134) or the self-important aristocratic father Mr Delvile in *Cecilia, or Memoirs of an Heiress* (1782). In *Camilla, or A Picture of Youth* (1796), she showed a young woman growing up to learn, not to function on her own, but to rely on the judgment of her elders even more than she had at first. In the same novel, Burney revealed in those respected elders the devastating effects of rigorous conventional virtue and narrow judgment. Painfully proper Juliet is matched in *The Wanderer* with Elinor, who is given free rein to question the foundations of patriarchal order.

I believe that any interpretation of Burney must take into account both the conformity that she consistently professed and the individualist protest that continually appears. Therefore I cannot agree with those who see her as 'a self-conscious social reformer' (Epstein 4), purposefully and wholeheartedly protesting against the norms of her society. Each of her novels reveals an uneasy mixture of social satire based on acceptance of the established order and subversive protest against it, reflected in tones that vary incongruously from those of poised comedy of manners to those of violent melodrama.[2]

But if these inconsistencies weaken the artistic effectiveness of her fiction, they do not interfere with her most distinctive contribution to the developing novel: her intense rendition of the psychological problems of women – problems that are characteristic of her own time, but are also perennial. As a perceptive, creative, energetic woman, she saw through pretentious authority and resented narrow restrictions. As an inhibited, conventional one, she suffered guilt and ambivalence, felt herself helpless before established authority, struggled to be self-effacing and blameless. Her novels do not present clear criticism, but rather the anxiety, the frustration, the painful ambivalence felt by women imprisoned in a patriarchal ideology which makes them suffer but which they are not equipped to challenge. Repeatedly, she set up reasonable expectations – that the heiress Cecilia will be able to organize her own life, that Camilla will satisfy the people whose approval she desperately tries to maintain, that Juliet will support herself in accordance with her firm resolution – and then showed how society and circumstance knock them down. She devised plots to illustrate the actual situation of women – enforced passivity, diminution in marriage, guilt from trying to meet conflicting demands, unavoidable dependence on others. She provided happy endings, rewarding her heroine with an ideal husband, and then undercut them by leaving unresolved the problems she had raised in the book.

Through her heroines, Burney enlarged and heightened her personal experiences of 'female difficulties' and thereby threw them into sharper focus. Cecilia, the beautiful heiress, has freedom and opportunities closed to Burney – yet she ends up equally controlled by the people around her. Burney was spared the trials that keep Camilla perpetually in the wrong – yet she expressed through this heroine the guilt that was imposed on both of them as a result of their circumstances as women.[3] The close relationship between fiction and fact – as both reflection and model – is exemplified by the reaction of three of Burney's heroines and the author herself to intolerable stress. As Burney got her father's permission to resign from her Court appointment by becoming so ill she thought she was dying, Evelina sickens when she believes the man she loves is unworthy and goes to a spa to recover, where they meet and all is explained. Cecilia is driven to delirium when no one will listen to her, and distress at her suffering causes both her husband and her father-in-law to appreciate her true worth. Similarly, Camilla sinks into delirium and near death when she believes she has lost her lover and ruined her father, and as a result everyone forgives her and there is a general reconciliation. In each case, stress leads the heroine to illness, and illness – aggression turned inward – enables her passively to manipulate others to get what she needs.

Burney's background offered exceptional opportunities, which were necessary for any woman to achieve intellectual distinction in the eighteenth century. At the same time, her close family ties created a pressing need to please those she loved that reinforced both her tendencies to comply and conform and her anxiety about achievement and publicity.

The overwhelming influence in Frances Burney's life was her father, Dr Charles Burney. An eminent music teacher and musicologist, he was also an exceptionally charming and sociable man. Although he took no active part in Frances's education, he set his children an example of self-cultivation and hard work. As their family friend Hester Thrale later remarked, the Burneys' 'Esteem & fondness for the Dr seems to inspire them all . . . & so every individual of it must write and read & be literary' (Piozzi, *Thraliana* 399). He appreciated the company of intelligent women; both his wives were witty and well read, and he was a favorite among the Bluestockings. He was too conventional, however, to approve of the classical languages for women, and he forbid Frances to learn Latin. As a self-made man, he was intent on preserving the family gentility; and he transmitted to Frances his concern for propriety and good breeding. He was a disarmingly sweet man, but ruthlessly self-centered and self-promoting.

Although he appreciated Frances's achievements, he considered them secondary to his own work and the social advancement of the family. His female relatives exerted themselves to protect him from unpleasant news, and he made this easy by his imperviousness to whatever he did not wish to hear. As Frances charitably put it: 'Dearest father! how blessed in that facility of believing all people as good and as happy as he wishes them!' (*DL* 3:159).

Dr Burney's charm, affection and egotism unfortunately combined to produce in his daughters a devotion so uncritical that they found it almost unbearable to displease him. At seventeen, Frances ascribed her life's happiness 'to my father! to this dearest, most amiable, this best beloved – most worthy of men! – it is his goodness to me which makes all appear so gay, it is his affection which makes *my* sun shine' (*ED* 1:46). At thirty-four, when she fully recognized the debilitating misery of her life at Court, she wrote to her sister Susanna:

> . . . nothing but my horror of disappointing, perhaps displeasing, my dearest father, has deterred me . . . from soliciting his leave to resign. But oh . . . kind, good, indulgent as is to me, I have not the heart so cruelly to thwart his hopes – his views – his happiness, in the honours he conceived awaiting my so unsolicited appointment. (*DL* 3:10)

This sacrifice of five miserable, unproductive years was the most baneful effect of Dr Burney's influence; but the pressure he exerted toward conventional propriety was pervasive. When Frances was over forty, he made her drop the friendship of Madame de Staël, whom she liked and admired, because he suspected de Staël's morals. And he did his best to prevent her marriage to Alexandre d'Arblay, an ideally congenial partner, because the match was imprudent (thus suggesting unseemly passion in Frances), and d'Arblay was French, Roman Catholic and mildly liberal in politics. Far from resenting her father's refusal to attend her wedding, she was deeply grateful when he became reconciled. Her need to retain the approval of this highly conventional man would have precluded any open defiance of convention in her novels. His influence is also seen in her heroines' excessive devotion to good father figures.

Frances's mother died when she was ten. The fact that she existed only as an idealized memory may have actually facilitated Frances's creative development. There does seem to be a correlation between motherlessness and female achievement in the eighteenth century. A large proportion of eighteenth-century women intellectuals, including Anne Finch, Charlotte Smith and Elizabeth Carter, lost their mothers in childhood; the mothers who survived either took no part in their daughters' scholarly or creative development or actively discouraged it. Since most women were forced into conventionality, the likelihood was that a mother would use her enormous emotional power to pressure her daughter into conformity with the passive self-abnegating feminine ideal of the time. Hester Thrale, by nature a far more self-assured woman than Burney, shows the blighting effects of devotion to a conventionally perfect mother. Although Hester was a brilliant and well-educated woman, her lifelong literary ambition produced scanty and disappointing results. Her personal life, also, showed an uneasy alternation between self-abnegation for others and resentment against them for accepting it. Apparently caught between the need to be an irreproachable traditional woman and the need to break out of that restrictive mold, Hester was unable to do either in a satisfactory and satisfying way.

She could not help admiring her mother, who was beautiful, impeccably aristocratic in manners, highly educated by contemporary standards and ready to sacrifice everything to what she considered her duty: namely, self-immolation in order to keep her undeserving husband satisfied and comfortable. The mother naturally educated her daughter in her own image, and Hester was unable to resist this training because of her love and veneration for a woman who seemed to her beyond criticism. Hester married an unsympathetic man to please her mother and resolutely strove to make him a devoted wife, regardless of his selfish unresponsiveness. She would never have been liberated at all had it not been for Samuel Johnson (whose influence her mother disapproved), who told her she could never hope to interest her husband if she did not stop submerging herself in infant care (as her mother exhorted) and start to develop herself. As a result, she became known as a brilliant hostess and conversationalist.

Burney, in contrast, had a stepmother she disliked. While she obeyed her, she remained free to resist her inwardly. If her stepmother thought that needlework was more proper for girls than intellectual pursuits, Frances could comfortably compromise by devoting her mornings to sewing and her afternoons to reading and writing (*ED* 1:15). Frances was not emotionally dependent on her approval and therefore did not feel guilty for not complying totally, in spirit and in letter, as she did with her father's wishes. It was next-to-impossible for her to resist authority figures whom she loved and respected; it was fortunate for her that she was able to wring consent, however ungracious, from the Queen to leave her service, and from her father to marry d'Arblay.

On the other hand, Burney could resent authority she thought abused. Arbitrary treatment even from the Queen could raise 'republican feelings' in her breast, although a civil question dispelled them at once (*DL* 3:99). When the authority was an unpleasant person like Mrs Schwellenberg, her immediate superior at Court, she could defend herself by acknowledging hostility and expressing it in the privacy of her journals, even though she shrank from confrontation. Tyrannical behavior by Schwellenberg caused her to 'grow *Democrate* at once.' 'Indeed,' she added, 'I feel always *democrate* where I think Power abused, – whether by the Great or the Little'

(*JL* 1:89). In defense of the well-being of someone she loved, Burney could even fight effectively. When a Prussian commandant stopped her progress to join her wounded husband at Trèves by arbitrarily refusing to sign her passport, she refused to leave until he did what she wanted: 'Brutality so unauthorized, however it shocked, I would not suffer to intimidate me' (*JL* 8:487).[4]

A disliked authority figure can even crystallize resistance; a stepmother who inveighed 'very frequently and seriously against the evil of a scribbling turn in young ladies – the loss of time, the waste of thought, in idle, crude inventions – and the . . . utter discredit of being known as a female writer of novels and romances' (*DL* 1:12) could provoke her to a rebellion of which she would otherwise not be capable.

Frances was supported in her revolt and in her creative efforts by a large, warm group of sisters, brothers and cousins. All the Burneys were witty and articulate, with a well-developed sense of fun. They wrote good letters, and several published books. Like the Austens and the Edgeworths, the Burneys formed an enthusiastic support group – an inestimable advantage for modest ladies in an age when women novelists might still be suspected as disreputable or egotistical. (The Duchess of Portland had 'a prejudice against female novel writers, which *almost* amounted to a *horror of them*,' and was with difficulty prevailed upon to let Burney be introduced to her; she consented because of the pure morality of *Cecilia* and the modesty of its author [qtd Hemlow 168].) However, the Burneys did not provide help in the form of salutary criticism. Dr Burney was loyally enthusiastic about his daughter's productions, but too undiscriminating to be helpful in improving their quality; he indignantly denied every criticism, including such justified charges as occasional tedium in *Camilla* (Hemlow 269).

Frances never went to school or had formal instruction. Spurred on solely by 'her unbounded veneration for the character, and affection for the person, of her father; who, nevertheles had not, at the time, a moment to spare for giving her any personal lessons, or even for directing her pursuits' (*Memoirs* 1:198), she educated herself. She did not learn to read until she was eight, presumably because of some problem with anxiety or repressed anger. But in her teens she put herself through an extensive reading program in her father's library. Considering her natural shyness and the narrowness of female education at the time, it may have been fortunate that she was left to develop in her own way.

Much of her education was social. Dr Burney's charm brought him a wide circle of friends, including the most distinguished people in London. A varied and often brilliant company regularly frequented the household. David Garrick, who was particularly fond of the Burney children, used to come by and entertain them with mimicry, and thus perhaps helped to develop Frances's own gift, which she put to good use in giving voices to her fictional characters. Other guests ranged from the great Samuel Johnson to fools, fops and vulgarians such as Burney pilloried in her novels. Right in her own home, she was provided with brilliance to imitate and a variety of follies to ridicule. Dr Burney also prepared her for professional writing by making her work as his secretary, copying and recopying his books on music. In this way, she became familiar with professional standards of style and composition and with the mechanics of publication.

His old friend Samuel Crisp contributed more directly to her creative development. Crisp was a man of keen intellect, knowledge of the world and fastidious taste, who had withdrawn from society to a country house at Chessington. He thus had leisure time to devote to the Burney children, of whom Frances was his favorite, as well as taste and knowledge to guide her writing. What he gave her intellectually is indicated by her report in her diary, at the age of eighteen: 'I have had to-day the first real conversation I ever had in my life, except with Mr. Crisp. . . . It was with Mr. Seaton' (*ED* 1:33). Moreover, when she visited him at Chessington, her time was more at her own disposal than at home; it was there she wrote much of both *Evelina* and *Cecilia*. Crisp was an avid reader of Frances's journals, in which she honed the talent for comic social reportage which forms the strength of her novels. Moreover, he read them critically: he urged her to 'Dash away' spontaneously and tried to discourage the prolixity and studied pomposity that perpetually threatened her style (*ED* 1:268, 279).

Frances had been secretly scribbling 'little works of invention' from the age of ten. Her sister Susanna's affectionate praises 'rendered the stolen moments of their secret readings the happiest of their adolescent lives.' At the same time, she always felt guilty about her writing and several times tried to stop. On her fifteenth birthday, she burned all her manuscripts (including the history of Caroline Evelyn, Evelina's mother), while she and Susanna wept over the bonfire; and she resolved 'to extinguish for ever in their ashes her scribbling propensity' (*Memoirs* 2:123–5).

The next year, however, she started a diary, which, significantly, she addressed to 'Nobody.' In a journal, she felt,

> I must imagion myself to be talking – talking to the most intimate of friends . . . but who must this friend be? . . . to *whom* dare I reveal my private opinion of my nearest relations? my secret thoughts of my dearest friends? my own hopes, fears, reflections, and dislikes? Nobody! . . . to Nobody can I be wholly unreserved. . . . The love, the esteem I entertain for Nobody, Nobody's self has not power to destroy. . . . From Nobody I have nothing to fear. . . . In your breast my errors may create pity without exciting contempt; may raise your compassion, without eradicating your love. From this moment, then, my dear girl – but why, permit me to ask, must a *female* be made Nobody? (*ED* 1:5·6)

She wants both to express and to conceal: she sees her diary as communication to a friend, yet she does not want to reveal her opinions and feelings to anyone; quite literally, 'to Nobody can I be wholly unreserved.' At the same time, 'Nobody' is a fictive person to whom she is writing – namely, herself. The playful conceit well expresses her ambivalence: in the very act of asserting herself by starting to formulate her feelings and opinions in writing, she effaces herself by calling herself 'Nobody.' She can simultaneously boldly assert her self-esteem, which nobody has power to destroy, and protect herself from criticism by denying it. She can pardon her own errors, or perhaps nobody can pardon them. Finally, by abruptly bringing in the reference to her sex, she indicates her awareness and resentment of society's particular disapproval of self-assertion in women. Her first-person narrator Evelina also asserts herself against society's dismissal by resentfully calling herself 'Nobody' when the aristocratic snobs at Mrs Beaumont's house act as if she were not there (289).

Burney's apprehensions about self-expression were not entirely self-created. An early episode in her diary shows her father's subtle encouragement of her guilt feelings, as well as her own liability to guilt. One day she inadvertently left a page of her journal in the parlor, where he found it. She fretted in suspense for over a day until, unable to stand any more, she asked him if he had any papers of hers. He asked her gravely why she left her papers about the house and continued to play the pianoforte for an hour and a half, during which time she half resolved 'never to write a word more.' At last he rose, noted her wistful look, laughed, and asked kindly, 'What, Fanny . . . are you in sad distress?' Then he relented and returned the paper, with a warning: 'take care, my dear, of leaving your writings about the house again – suppose any-body else had found it. . . . Here, take it – but if ever I find any more of your Journals, I vow I'll stick them up in the market place.' The prolonged teasing, superficially so kind and playful, was thoughtless if not sadistic; but Frances did not think so: 'And then he kiss'd me *so* kindly – never was parent so *properly*, so *well*-judgedly affectionate! I was so frightened that I have not had the heart to write since, till now [four days later], I should not but that – in short, but that I cannot help it! As to the *paper*, I destroy'd it the moment I got it' (*ED* 1:18–19).

It is a dramatic demonstration of the power of a revered father over a dutiful eighteenth-century daughter. Convinced of his wisdom and loving concern for her welfare, she was driven to anxious misery by fear of his disapproval. Unwittingly, he played on her native shyness and need to be perfectly proper, and thus increased them. One wonders why Burney felt so guilty about anyone's seeing what was no doubt an innocent journal entry. Leaving a private paper where anyone could find it did, of course, make her guilty of Camilla's sin, imprudence. But the intensity of her anxiety suggests guilt over the self-expression and self-assertion necessarily involved in writing – a guilt that could not be avoided because she could not stop writing. Though she could not avoid the 'guilt' of writing, this experience confirmed her fearfulness. Perhaps that is why imagination seemed so dangerous to her and why, when she developed her heroines' guilt in the realm of personal relations rather than creative self-expression, she connected emotional overindulgence with imagination.

While her father treated her diary-writing as an embarrassing secret, Dorothy Young, a well-meaning friend of the family, strongly warned her against keeping a diary at all. Young expressed her apprehensions in terms of sexuality – always the context for warnings to women in this period, and inextricably associated with self-assertion on their part. A diarist articulates feelings that should remain unknown and then writes them down where others might see them. Suppose Frances should feel a predilection for a young man . . . suppose she should confide this to her diary . . . suppose he should see the entry? Burney found the example devastating: there would be no recourse but a jump into Rosamond's Pond. Nevertheless, she persisted with her diary; and she succeeded in convincing Young that hers, at least, was pure of discreditable feelings (*ED* 1:19–21). It was vitally important that she continue writing, for her own mental health as well as for her future literary achievement. Trained to silence as most women were, personally shy as well, she needed to write in order to express, even to create, herself (Simons 115–16).

From the diary she progressed to journal-letters to Susanna; soon Crisp was clamoring to see them and asking permission to send copies to his sister. For the rest of her life, she kept voluminous journals, which came to be circulated among an appreciative group of family and friends. Through them, she maintained 'a sense of emotional relationship with her readers,' those few people whose approval and understanding she required (Straub 154). The experience of writing to an appreciative audience helped to give her confidence to write a novel for publication.

Burney seems to have taken care to present in her journals an acceptable version of herself, one who could not be faulted on grounds of feminine morality or ladylike decorum, one who was always refined and never critical of conventional wisdom. What bulks the largest is reportage of social scenes, where most often she silently observes or responds to others' initiatives. When she does mention her feelings, they are consistent with decorum – she is comically embarrassed by shyness which she cannot help, derisive of obvious vulgarity or stupidity, indignant at authority that is usurped, admiring of recognized excellence. She is never passionate or explicitly self-assertive; she never bares feelings that might discredit her. She may criticize individual foolish men for patronizing or bullying women, but she never challenges the patriarchal order, as, for instance, Lady Mary Wortley Montagu did in several letters to her daughter;[5] she never openly suggests that injustice toward women was built into the institutions of her society.

In the early diary she occasionally permits herself to question convention, but even there, she qualifies and retreats. She admires her stepsister Maria Allen's sincerity in openly showing her contempt for fools, but then says 'she pays too little regard to the world.' She suggests that Maria should be praised for breaking 'through the confinement of custom . . . [to] shew the way to a new and open path,' then blames 'severity to *harmless* folly, which claims pity and not scorn,' but finally 'cannot but acknowledge it to be infinitely tiresome, and for any length of time even almost disgustful' (*ED* 1:134). Despite her unusually strong distaste for uncongenial company, she cannot assert even to herself that a woman should be able to violate conventional decorum by revealing unpleasing judgments of people. In a similar passage, she complains of the waste of time in visiting with people she has no interest in seeing; recognizes that such formal socializing is motivated neither by affection nor desire to please, but only custom; remarks that 'we all blame – and all obey' custom, 'without knowing why or wherefore – which keeps our better reason, which sometimes dares to shew it's folly, in subjection' – and concludes by dismissing her entire argument as 'a very ridiculous affair' (*ED* 1:54; Spacks, *Imagining a Self: Autobiography and Novel in Eighteenth Century England* 163).

Burney's writing of *Evelina* (1778) illustrates the discouraging working conditions of eighteenth-century women authors. First, she had to find time for writing when her father did not require her services as his secretary. Then, she felt the need to write it in secret, although she gradually confided in Susanna and other members of the family. She moved quickly through the first draft, but the second – involving revision and fair copying for the printer – went more slowly. Because of the secrecy, she had to stay up at night in unheated rooms to write it. Moreover, she had the added strain of disguising her handwriting; for she feared that it might be recognized from her work on her father's manuscripts and dreaded disgracing him by association with a work that might prove unworthy. She approached a publisher (through her younger brother Charles) and was crushed to learn that he would not accept the first two volumes without the third. This seemed a small thing to him, but to her, who had to do her writing late at night, the difficulty seemed insuperable. 'Now, this man, knowing nothing of my situation, supposed, in all probability, that I could seat myself quietly at my bureau, and write on with all expedition and ease, till the work was finished. But . . . I had hardly time to write half a page in a day; and neither my health nor inclination would allow me to continue my *nocturnal* scribbling for so long a time, as to write first, and then copy, a whole volume. I was therefore obliged to give the attempt and affair entirely over for the present.' Fortunately, she was soon allowed to pay a long visit to Chessington, where 'every body is disengaged, and at liberty to pursue their own inclinations' (*ED* 2:162). There she managed to finish the novel before she had to hurry off to visit her uncle, lest he feel slighted.

Burney virtuously abstained from complaining about the drains on her time, but another struggling novelist, Laetitia Hawkins, daughter of Sir John Hawkins, a contemporary and rival historian of music, thus described her difficulties in doing her own work: 'I was, I will not say *educated*, but *broke*, to the drudgery of my father's pursuits. I had no time but what I could *purloin* from my incessant task of copying, or writing from dictation – writing six hours in the day for my father, and reading nearly as long to my mother' (*ED* 1:lxviii).

Dr Burney learned the authorship of *Evelina*, from Susanna, only after the book had turned out to be a brilliant success. Everyone was reading it, and all who read were enthusiastic. Still, although Frances enjoyed hearing her characters praised, she found direct references to her authorship indelicate. She suspected that writing might be egotistically self-indulgent and realistic comedy ungenteel. 'An *Authoress*,' she worried, 'must always be supposed to be flippant, assuming & loquacious' (qtd Hemlow 63). When Thrale was to be told that she had written *Evelina*, Burney was afraid she would wonder 'where I can have kept company, to describe such a family as the Branghtons, Mr. Brown, and some others? Indeed (thank Heaven!), I don't myself recollect ever passing half an hour at a time with any *one* person *quite* so bad; so that, I am afraid she will conclude I must have an innate vulgarity of ideas, to assist me with such coarse colouring for the objects of my imagination' (*DL* 1:37). Although she recognized the truth of Thrale's charge that it was inconsistent to publish a book and then shrink from being known, she was sickened by anxiety: 'notwithstanding all her advice, and all her encouragement, I was so much agitated by the certainty of being known as a scribbler, that I was really ill all night, and could not sleep' (*DL* 1:97).

Even more significantly, her success inspired her with fear:

> I am now at the summit of a high hill; my prospects on one side are bright, glowing, and invitingly beautiful; but when I turn round, I perceive, on the other side, sundry caverns, gulphs, pits, and precipices, that, to look at, make my head giddy and my heart sick . . . if I move, it must be downwards. I have already, I fear, reached the pinnacle of my abilities, and therefore to stand still will be my best policy. But there is nothing under heaven so difficult to do. Creatures who are formed for motion *must* move, however great their inducements to forbear.

She went on ingeniously to find reasons why a second novel could not find the favor *Evelina* had (*DL* 1:40–1). It is a striking example of the female fear of success which has been identified in our own time. Yet even as she expresses her apprehensions, she recognizes that her creative energy is too strong to quench.

Her first attempt after *Evelina* served to confirm her apprehensions. Discerning readers had noticed her gift for vivid, natural-sounding comic dialogue and thought she could easily adapt it to the theater. This move would be highly advisable for one who needed money, and Burney was twenty-six years old and unmarried; she lacked the key assets of exceptional beauty or fortune, and her father could not support her indefinitely. Generally speaking, successful plays were far more profitable than novels; Thrale pointed out that Hannah More had got nearly four hundred pounds for her mediocre tragedy *Percy*. Two highly successful dramatists, Arthur Murphy and Richard Brinsley Sheridan, then the manager of the Drury Lane Theatre, personally urged Burney to write a play and assured her of their help.

In view of her obvious talent and the strong support offered her, the fiasco of the resulting play illustrates both her own ambivalence about achievement and publicity and her mentors' subtle, unwitting discouragement. *The Witlings* is a hilariously funny play, but Burney's choice of subject was singularly perverse, since the main object of satire is intellectual women. What was more evidently self-destructive at the time was that the major butt, Elizabeth Montagu, was the most powerful Bluestocking hostess and had been very gracious to Burney. Her justified fury, had the play been produced, would have destroyed Burney's favored, but precarious, social position. It is possible that Burney was not consciously attacking Montagu, whose worst enemies could not have accused her of the gross ignorance displayed by Lady Smatter; but the character's bossiness, conceit, wealth and dependent nephew would have immediately suggested the great hostess.

Dr Burney and Crisp were alarmed by this imprudence, but conveyed their reservations mainly in the form of dark insinuations of indelicacy. These cannot be taken at face value, since *The Witlings* is totally innocent of sexual suggestiveness. Possibly Crisp was thinking of the publicity of theatrical representation or the bawdiness of earlier (though certainly not contemporary) comedy. Anyway, somehow, writing for the stage was not compatible with the utmost degree of feminine delicacy. This hint was enough for Frances, who dreaded above all things risking 'ridicule or censure as a female' (*DL* 1:162). With pathetic regrets, she suppressed *The Witlings*.

This episode illustrates the way a woman can cooperate in her own restriction. Burney did shrink from publicity and dreaded unfavorable notice, as it might affect herself or her father: 'I cannot get out of my head the idea of disgracing so many people' (*DL* 1:131). As Crisp recognized, her spirit was 'already too diffident and apprehensive' (*DL* 1:321). Hence he and her father were genuinely responding to her vulnerability. At the same time, they used it to protect their own standards of propriety in a woman connected with them. They were simultaneously restricting and protecting her; her creative efforts were being stifled, but she was willingly participating in that process.

The same pattern of obscurely motivated discouragement complemented by her own defeatism dogged Burney's several later attempts to write for the stage. The only play she actually had produced was *Edwy and Elgiva* (1795), a dreary tragedy that she had written during her most unhappy time at Court; it was, as the actors had predicted, a humiliating failure and was withdrawn after one night. In 1800, she wrote *Love and Fashion*, an amusing, conventional comedy that, given her connections, should have been successful and profitable. Again, however, her father blocked her enterprise. It is not clear why – whether he was genuinely concerned for her feelings (she was still painfully shy and had suffered over the failure of *Edwy and Elgiva*), or snobbishly unwilling to see his daughter associated with the stage, or ambivalent about her career. This time, Frances did allow herself a delicate note of reproach in the letter she wrote to announce the withdrawal of the play, already in rehearsal: although she assured her father she knew that his goodness, kindness and 'regard for my fame' were what caused his trepidation, she found 'unaccountable' his displeasure at her 'doing what I have all my life been urged to, & all my life intended, writing a Comedy' (*JL* 4:394–5). All discussion ceased, however, when Frances was prostrated by the death of Susanna, which, she said, marked the end of her 'perfect Happiness on Earth' (qtd Hemlow 291).

Nevertheless, she made two further attempts. *A Busy Day*, which comically exploits class differences in the manner of *Evelina*, has been called her best play, although it lacks the satiric bite of *The Witlings*. Finally, she tried to salvage *The Witlings* by revising it into *The Woman Hater*. But she did not attempt to get either of them produced. Burney's frustrating and self-defeating relationship with the theater is hard to explain. She obviously had the requisite talent, and her unproduced comedies meet all the criteria for success in the theater of her day. She had incomparable connections, with men such as Sheridan and Murphy ready to help her with dramaturgy and promotion. She certainly needed the money, more than she could make from novels. By her time, highly respectable women like Frances Sheridan were regularly writing for the stage. And yet she wrote her first play on a theme that would offend powerful patrons; she repeatedly let herself be dissuaded from production by patently inadequate arguments; the one play she did have produced was the obvious loser *Edwy and Elgiva*. Perhaps her guilt over authorship – overcome by her need to express herself in the case of novels and journals – asserted itself by drawing the line at stage comedy, of which her mentors disapproved.

Both Dr Burney and Crisp pressed Frances to capitalize on the success of *Evelina* with another novel, primarily for financial reasons. She quoted to her father Crisp's opinion 'that it would be the best policy, but for pecuniary advantages, for me to write no more' after *Evelina*, and went on to state that she agreed with it (*DL* 1:258). Despite its success, *Evelina* had brought in only twenty guineas, because the young Burneys were too inexperienced to negotiate effectively with a publisher. However, her elders gave her the mixed signals which women so often get with regard to achievement. At the same time that they admired her talent and urged her to exploit it, they pushed her into social engagements that took up the time she needed to write.[6] She was pressured into publishing *Cecilia* prematurely, before she had time to revise it thoroughly. In particular, as she herself recognized, she did not retrench her natural prolixity.

Nevertheless, the book was greatly admired and highly successful. Its success did not earn her financial security, however. Her father, with all his experience as a professional writer, negotiated a publishing agreement that was not much better than the one she had accepted for *Evelina*: Payne and Cadell bought the copyright for two hundred and fifty pounds, which was invested to produce an income of twenty pounds a year. According to Frances's sister Charlotte, most people thought she should have got a thousand pounds (*ED* 2:307). Ironically, the plot of *Cecilia* turns on the mismanagement of a young woman's money.

Crisp's reaction throws light on why Dr Burney did not drive a better bargain. Crisp thought the price was perfectly adequate, since all Frances had to do was 'sit by a warm Fire and in 3 or 4 months . . . gain £250 by scribbling the Inventions of her own Brain – only putting down in black and white whatever comes into her own head, without labour drawing singly from her own Fountain' (qtd Hemlow 148). Despite his sincere enthusiasm, he could not take this complex, weighty novel seriously: it flowed spontaneously, and therefore did not merit a professional price, like a work requiring judgment, a history of music, for example. Besides, he no doubt thought of her earnings as pin money. And yet the plain fact was that she had the same need of support a man had and, as an unmarried woman from a family of limited means, the same responsibility to support herself.

That her work was not taken seriously was indicated more disastrously by the offer that now came to her and brought delight to her father and most of her friends. Through Mary Delany, who was a personal friend of the royal family, she met King George and Queen Charlotte, who offered her the post of Second Keeper of the Robes to the Queen. This was a signal distinction, especially for one who had no high family connections; and her acquaintance assumed she would accept it joyfully as an honorable lifetime settlement. But Frances realized what kind of life it would mean. She would be in constant attendance, every day, from early morning until late at night; her duties would be boring and menial – mixing snuff, running errands, passing jewels, standing around in case she should be wanted; she would be expected to socialize constantly with people of her grade at Court, regardless of her preferences; and she would have no opportunity to stay with friends or relatives or even to receive visitors except with special permission.

For a woman whose peace, cheerfulness and 'every chance of felicity' rested 'totally and solely upon enjoying the society, the confidence, & the kindness of those I esteem & love' (qtd Hemlow 236), this isolation was the worst deprivation of all. In a society where amiable women were supposed to adapt themselves to whatever social setting they were placed in, Burney found superficial socializing positively offensive. She could 'go nowhere with pleasure or spirit, if I meet not somebody who interests my heart as well as my head' (*DL* 2:253).

Nevertheless, Frances could not bear to disappoint her father. She did not tell him how she felt, nor even make her reluctance clear to her sisters, who would have passed on the information. Her new life proved to be even more oppressive than she had anticipated. Unable to resist or complain – for she soon developed an excessive regard for the Queen's feelings comparable to what she felt for her father's – she could only withdraw into herself and ruthlessly suppress her inclinations. She wrote to Susanna that she planned 'to wean myself from myself – to lessen all my affections – to curb all my wishes – to deaden all my sensations' (*DL* 3:9). It was an appalling resolve for a gifted, fun-loving woman of thirty-four, revealing the hold of repressive, self-immolating morality upon her.

In the eyes of society, a woman was better employed in waiting on the Queen than in writing first-class novels. No one, apparently, saw the incongruity of a best-selling novelist's having to take work she hated in order to support herself. That Burney could have supported herself by her writing is proven by her profits from *Camilla*, written after her escape from Court and her marriage. Since her husband could not pursue his military career in England and a child was coming, it was up to her to augment the family's income. Finally comfortable with the idea of using her talent as a financial resource, since it would benefit others, she agreed to publish *Camilla* by subscription, the best way to maximize profits. She also dedicated it to the Queen, which promoted its sales. Altogether, between subscription, royal present and sales, Burney cleared about two thousand pounds; and the d'Arblays were able to build themselves a house, 'Camilla Cottage.'

I

EVELINA: Or, The History of a Young Lady's Entrance into the World

EVELINA: or The History of a Young Lady's Entrance into the World vividly presents experiences familiar to any young woman, together with sharply comic social satire and sentimental appeal. The combination remains potent today, and it was enchantingly new to the readers of 1778. For the first time, an easily recognizable young woman was expressing herself in fiction. Richardson's heroines are separated from the reader by their extraordinary circumstances and merits; one cannot identify directly with the paragon Clarissa, and even Harriet Byron's adventures are heightened well beyond normal experience (*Clarissa, or The History of a Young Lady*, 1747–8; *The History of Sir Charles Grandison*, 1753–4). The authors who presented young ladies in everyday life, entering the world as Evelina does, were not able to develop their feelings convincingly. Charlotte Lennox's Arabella (*The Female Quixote*, 1752), characterized mainly by her delusion that life is a chivalric romance, is amusing but far-fetched; Eliza Haywood's Betsy Thoughtless (1751) has such underdeveloped feelings that her efforts to attain a satisfactory life for herself make her seem crass and shallow.

But Evelina is lifelike and engaging as she goes through experiences familiar to female adolescents in her own time and ours. We have all suffered acutely from embarrassment at not knowing what to say when we particularly wish to shine, from mortification at being ignored in a social gathering or being caught in a party of unpresentable people, from self-delusion in refusing to recognize our attraction to a man even while we betray it by constantly speculating about him. Perceptive as she is about most things, Evelina reveals amusing obtuseness when she wonders that Sir Clement Willoughby, a rival young man, never happens to mention Lord Orville (157). She is more convincingly young than Lennox's and Haywood's heroines, partly because Burney presents her adolescent heroine's experience through her own eyes.[7]

Evelina is placed in a social setting that is solid and entertaining, she interacts with a wide variety of characters, and courtship is not the whole of her life. But her world is distinctively a young lady's world: it is one in which women are forced into passivity and men constantly encroach on their territory. In the novel's first significant scene, Evelina sits in a ballroom, while men saunter up and down, eyeing her and deciding whether it is worth their while to ask her to dance. Her choice, meanwhile, is between accepting the first man who offers or abstaining from dancing altogether. Since she does not yet understand woman's assigned role, she takes it on herself to reject the fop Mr Lovel and to accept Lord Orville; she pays for this violation of the rules with prolonged embarrassing consequences and learns that she had better not take similar decisive actions in future (Simons 52–4).[8] Throughout the novel, Evelina is eyed, grabbed, and coveted by men; and, being properly feminine – that is, innocent and gentle – she has no way to protect herself. When Willoughby has decoyed her alone with him into his carriage, she cannot deal with the situation because she cannot know whether he intends to rape her, to seduce her or to flirt playfully as he takes her home (Staves 371); it is fortunate for her that he relents. On repeated similar occasions, she must be protected from men by other men or by a 'masculine' woman like Mrs Selwyn.

Every man in the book except Lord Orville and her idealized guardian Mr Villars attempts to impose his will upon Evelina, and even Orville controls the terms of their relationship; for she cannot take any initiative to find out whether he loves her. Despite the importance of marriage to almost all women, they could not move freely through society to find a congenial man, nor could they even show serious interest in one before a proposal was actually made and approved by their parents. Usually their only choice was the one Evelina had in the ballroom, between acceptance of what was offered and refusal, which for most of them would mean poverty, emotional repression and society's disdain. Evelina, as a naïve observer, wonders what could have induced Mrs Mirvan to accept the Captain and why the family is glad he has come home. Her position is eminently reasonable, but a person better acquainted with the world would have known that the marriage was acceptable by the usual eighteenth-century standards, for the Captain is rich and of good family; he supports his wife and daughter and does not physically abuse them. And Mrs Mirvan only fulfills a wife's expected duty in overlooking her husband's faults and putting up a decorous facade.[9]

Women were forced to be passive and admired for being 'soft' – a favorite complimentary word with Burney herself, which she applied to female paragons like Mrs Delany. This encouraged men to be selfish: if women could not make their wishes felt, then only men's wishes needed to be considered; if men were the only people who could take the initiative, it was men's ends that were pursued. The results could be benign, like Lord Orville's patronage and then courtship of Evelina. But more often, men's privileged position resulted in bullying, crude sexual compliments or pawing, pursuit with the aim of seduction or enforced marriage.

The most entertaining aspect of *Evelina* is its social satire, a skillful adaptation of the wit–witwould–witless pattern of the Restoration comedy of manners to the later eighteenth-century scene. Orville and Willoughby effortlessly manipulate the social forms of courtship, while Lovel and Smith ludicrously fail; Captain Mirvan is a booe, but he can deflate Lovel's pretensions. Evelina herself can be a comic object in her inability to handle social situations, but she is a true wit in her discernment of follies, including her own. Her first meeting with Orville develops a comic contrast between his accomplished politeness and her inability to sustain the most ordinary conversation; the comedy is sharpened by her mortified awareness that she is looking like a fool and cannot manage to exert her normal intelligence. This awareness prevents her from enjoying his pleasantries about other guests and strikes her dumb when it occurs to her that he is politely trying different subjects in order to find out whether she is capable of talking upon *any* (32).

Burney's feminine point of view gives the manners comedy a distinctive new focus and additional depth. Evelina shrinks from Mirvan's macho crudity, sees through Smith's poor imitation of sophisticated gallantry, and is unable to deal with Willoughby's more artful courtship. She acutely distinguishes between genuine and exploitative gallantry: Orville's attentiveness shows his respect and consideration for her, while Willoughby's is an assertion of ownership (330).

Burney artfully plays off more against less subtle forms of bad manners. Young Branghton crudely jeers at women, but Mr Smith's self-congratulatory deference to the ladies' presumed wishes is equally contemptuous. The Branghtons artlessly make plain their disregard for each other's feelings, but the aristocrats' politeness is a thin disguise for equal indifference. When Lady Louisa complains that Lord Merton, her fiancé, has terrified her by his reckless driving and coquettishly confesses to having scolded him all morning, he answers, while 'twisting his whip with his fingers,' 'You have been, as you always are . . . all sweetness.'

Trying to provoke him into a warmer declaration, she proceeds: 'O fie, my Lord . . . I know you don't think so; I know you think me very ill-natured; – don't you, my Lord?' This moves him to reply: 'No, upon my honour; – how can your Ladyship ask such a question? Pray how goes time? my watch stands [i.e. is stopped]' (280). Louisa is herself a mistress of conveying disregard for others, as she casts 'her languishing eyes round the room, with a vacant stare, as if determined, though she looked, not to see who was in it' (285). Unlike her Restoration predecessors, Burney convincingly brings out the moral aspect of manners: rudeness, whether from the Branghtons or the aristocrats, results from unconcern for other people; and the less powerful the person – a young woman of uncertain social status, for example – the more apt are her feelings to be disregarded.

Long before the feminist analysis of Mary Wollstonecraft, who scornfully dismissed 'the trivial attentions which men think it manly to pay to the sex, when in fact, they are insultingly supporting their own superiority' (*Vindication* 147), Burney demonstrated that the gallant language that men think displays their good breeding and their respect for the ladies is in fact a thin cover for contempt. As Lovel asks for the honor and happiness of dancing with Evelina, it is clear that he expects her to feel honored. Willoughby professes total devotion in the very act of embarrassing and frightening her. Immediately after rudely slighting her in company, Lord Merton expects her to be flattered by his compliments.[10]

Even the peerless Lord Orville's politeness can be patronizing. Because he does not think it is worth his while to defend the value of operas against Captain Mirvan's rough challenge, Orville turns to the young ladies for their opinion. He says very nicely that the men have lost the benefit of the ladies' observations (109), but it is obvious that he is including the ladies because he is polite, not because he is interested in what they might have to say. Willoughby uses gallantry for the more sinister purpose of seduction; his mastery of the language of courtship gives him an unfair advantage in a game that could ruin Evelina's life. In the scene at the public assembly, we can enjoy his clever manipulation of manners and her embarrassed awkwardness on one level, while at the same time we notice his unscrupulous exploitation of her inexperience. Burney also shows how women contribute to the nominal chivalry that trivializes them: in the interchanges between Lady Louisa and the fashionable men, their undiscriminating compliments encourage her to practice the inanity and weakness that justify their contempt.

In general, Burney's social satire in *Evelina* is funny, pointed and meaningful. She intensifies real speech and manners without exaggerating them beyond belief, and she exposes the origin of bad manners in vanity and lack of feeling. Sometimes, however, her attacks misfire because of excess – extreme exaggeration of follies, belaboring of obvious butts, or inappropriately violent farce. Not only are Madame Duval and Captain Mirvan too crude to be amusing, but their relationship degenerates into physical abuse that is intrinsically unlikely and makes no satiric point. Beating an elderly woman and leaving her tied up in a ditch is not funny, nor is it an appropriate punishment for her rude self-assertiveness, nor does it throw light on the subjection of women. If Burney's point was that it was acceptable to bully women in her society, she had already made it far more convincingly through the long-suffering Mrs Mirvan, who spends her life accommodating to her brutish husband.

Such disproportionate punishment of a comic butt reveals a need to release hostility in an acceptable way. A woman of keen intellect and strong will who submitted to pervasive restriction, Burney necessarily accumulated repressed anger, which spilled out into whatever channels she permitted herself. Everyone would have recognized that an unfeminine, vulgar, selfish woman was a proper object of attack. Burney's need to express anger and scorn, together with her inhibitions about where it could be directed, sometimes cause her to lose artistic control in mocking a permissible target, so that hostility is more evident than instruction or diversion.

In a parallel case in real life, she reported at length the callous teasing of a young woman who appears to have been mildly retarded – 'not an absolute idiot; but . . . the verriest *booby* I ever knew.' Miss W—'s blunders kept everyone laughing, and she joined in because she did not understand that she was the butt. During dinner, Sir Herbert piqued himself 'upon *shewing her off*' and made 'ridiculous comments upon everything' she said; everyone else, including Burney, sneered or tittered. After supper, they all pressed Miss W— to sing. She protested that she could not, but they persuaded her. Her performance was ludicrous, and, after a brief attempt at restraint, Burney joined in the general merriment. Despite the bursts of laughter and increasingly provoking interruptions from Sir Herbert, who finally stuck a large spoon down her front, Miss W— persisted with her song. The next day, she poured out awkward confidences to Burney, not minding her laughter because Burney assured her it was not directed at her. Burney does not tire of exclaiming over her stupidity (*ED* 2:202–9). It is cheap and pointless fun.

Mr Dubster in *Camilla* is treated in the same way. Burney's repeated attacks on him become tiresome, because no one in or out of the book takes his pretensions seriously; it is neither amusing nor useful to reiterate that he is a vulgar *nouveau riche* who does not know his place. Hence her attack on him appears to be a mere exercise in snobbery, especially since she implies a natural connection between ill breeding and cruel insensitivity: he rejoices in having buried two rich wives, so that he can enjoy their money without themselves. No more than a compound of unattractive characteristics, he lacks the good humor of Mr Briggs, the common sense of Mr Hobson, or the kindness of Mr Tedman (*nouveaux riches* in *Cecilia* and *The Wanderer*). She uses him to make the same point she did with the Branghtons, but at greater and unnecessary length; and she does not engage him entertainingly with other characters, as she does Hobson.

In one painfully long-drawn scene, Lionel inveigles his

sisters Camilla and Eugenia to see Dubster's new house. Dubster takes them proudly around, showing them detail after detail that is cheap and in poor taste. Finally he takes them to his half-finished summer house, which can be reached only by a ladder. Lionel, in a characteristically outrageous practical joke, runs away with the ladder, leaving his sisters and Dubster stranded for hours. During this time, some laboring women come by and shout insults at Eugenia, who is deformed. There is no humor or satiric point here; and, although Burney expresses horror at the taunting of a cripple, she seems to be doing precisely that in having set up this scene in the first place.

Directed at an appropriate object, however, Burney's hostility could energize brilliant satiric exposure. *Cecilia*, probing into society and character as *Evelina* did not pretend to do, affords opportunities for weightier attack on fools who control the lives of more sensible people. Burney's ruthlessly protracted attack on old Mr Delvile in *Cecilia* is justified by the power and prestige he wields. Because he occupies a powerful and respected position in society, because many people would accept him at his own complacent evaluation, it is important to deflate him. Delvile is sublimely convinced that he is an important, a superior and a busy person. Why? – because he is accustomed to being deferred to. He talks constantly of being 'overwhelmed with business,' but that business typically consists of giving a few directions to his servants (516). He believes himself surrounded by 'people who can do nothing without my orders' (429), when in fact everyone wishes he would stay out of their way. Every occasion prompts him to proclaim a self-importance so complete that he cannot perceive other people's reactions. His dignity is the 'constant object of his thoughts and his cares' (456).

Although he constantly parades his generous condescension in troubling himself to be Cecilia's guardian, he invariably finds some reason not to be of any use to her. When she begs him to help her get rid of Sir Robert Floyer, who is persecuting her to accept him as a husband and is abetted by her other guardian Harrel, Delvile can think only that Harrel's behaviour

> has by no means been such as to lead me to forget that his father was the son of a steward of Mr. Grant, who lived in the neighbourhood of my friend and relation the Duke of Derwent: . . . The impropriety [of the Dean, Cecilia's uncle, in associating him with Harrel and Briggs] . . . has never obliterated from my mind the esteem I bore the Dean: nor can I possibly give a greater proof of it than the readiness I have always shewn to offer my counsel and instruction to his niece. Mr. Harrel, therefore, ought certainly to have desired Sir Robert Floyer to acquaint me with his proposals before he gave to him any answer. (307)

That is the beginning and the end of the help he offers.

Delvile's intelligent wife deals with him by avoiding him as much as possible, opposing him 'in nothing when his pleasure was made known,' but forbearing 'to enquire into his opinion except in case of necessity' (462). And yet all the while, he never doubts that he enjoys the same awe-filled deference from her and his son that he expects from the lower orders. He is surprised even more than aggrieved when his wife urges him to consent to their son's marriage to Cecilia: 'I had been willing to hope the affair over from the time my disapprobation of it was formally announced.' He threatens Mortimer with his 'eternal displeasure' if he attempts to discuss this subject further: 'it is no news, I flatter myself, to Mortimer Delvile or his mother, that I do nothing without reason' (818–19). In fact, he does nothing *with* reason: everyone around him can see that he is too governed by prejudice and emotion to be capable of clear thinking. Through Delvile, Burney undermines the moral foundation of patriarchy: namely, that senior males are more rational than women or young people, so that it is for everyone's good that they govern society. She shows, in contrast, how intelligent powerless people have to maneuver around stupid, selfish authorities in order to make them behave decently.

Burney misses no opportunity to contrast Delvile's pretensions to awesomeness with his actual inability to impress anyone, nor to show his pomposity deflated by his own need to assert his dignity. Mr Briggs is low, but he has business ability and self-respect based upon it; and he easily exposes the hollowness of a superiority based solely upon external advantages.[11] Even foolish Mrs Belfield can reduce Delvile to infuriated sputtering (778–86). The satire is pointed by the fact that he is offended as a result of his own pride, for if he had not arrogantly refused to tell her his name, she would never have repeated unflattering rumors about the Delviles to him. Whether Briggs is purposely insulting him or Hobson is merely addressing him as a fellow man, Delvile can respond only by pompously reasserting his superiority. Burney condemns him morally, but also – what is more effective – reduces him to absurd insignificance and ineffectuality.

In a novel where too many of the satiric butts mechanically repeat their comic turns, Delvile is consistently amusing because he is a solidly realized character. Burney exposes the basis for his arrogance and shows how his egotism manifests itself in various situations and relationships. He is sufficiently developed to have the virtues of his vices and to be capable of realistic changes of attitude. His family pride contributes to his genuine love for his son, on whom the continuation of the family depends. The very pride that caused him to misjudge and reject Cecilia when he had convinced himself that she was unworthy forces him to repent when he can no longer justify his actions to himself. When he learned that his hard-hearted refusal to credit her marriage almost precipitated her death, 'Neither his dignity nor his displeasure had been able to repress remorse, a feeling to which, with all his foibles, he had not been accustomed,' and he must allay it by accepting her (928). He continues to treat her with respect because she is his son's wife (931).

In ridiculing Delvile, Burney used her anger constructively, directing it at an appropriate target and tempering it with artistry. Unlike Madame Duval, Delvile represents personal and political power assured of its superiority. Burney's artistic control appears in his humanizing features, such as love for his son and regard to the obligations of his rank, and the inventiveness with which she develops his absurdities: we wonder how he will display his arrogance in each new situation.

As Burney's hostility to Delvile is controlled by her clearly defined satiric purpose, her hostility to Briggs is balanced by affection: his pathological stinginess does not become oppressive because she endows him with good humor and freedom from pretense. With the more fully developed Sir Hugh Tyrold of *Camilla*, her hostility almost disappears in affection. Her triumph lies in making equally convincing Sir Hugh's goodness and his folly, in making us respect his kindness at the same time that we laugh at his way of expressing it. Burney plays off Sir Hugh's hopeless dullness against the sterile pedantry of his learned protégé Dr Orkborne. When the patron plans a pleasant surprise for the scholar by having his books placed in new bookcases and his study cleaned, and Orkborne bursts into a passion because a blotted page of notes has been destroyed, Orkborne's self-importance about his useless work contrasts delightfully with the ignorance of scholarly priorities that Sir Hugh shares equally with his servants (209–11).

All Sir Hugh's blunders come from his good heart, and he repents for every one with the same gentle incomprehension of where he has gone wrong. He is always ludicrously misjudging people, but it is because he sees them in his own kindly image. He takes pains to avoid hurting the feelings of people like Orkborne, not seeing that Orkborne is too self-absorbed to notice whether anyone is disapproving of him (40). He misses the most obvious sarcasm or ungracious consent because he takes 'everything literally that seemed right or good-natured' (186). When hostility is so blatant that he is absolutely forced to recognize it, his reaction nicely balances muddled thinking with intuitive insight and an instinctive repugnance to uncharity. Too sweet and unassuming to censure anyone, he merely remarks, after a pert schoolboy has mocked his incapacity to learn Latin:

> I had as lieve see him a mere dunce all his life, supposing I should live so long, which God forbid in regard to his dying, as have him turn out a mere coxcomb of a pedant, laughing and grinning at everybody that can't spell a Greek noun. (43)

Burney simultaneously evokes laughter and moves to sympathy, more effectively than she moves in her pathetic set scenes.

She brilliantly expresses Sir Hugh's muddled thought processes in his manner of speaking, as when he says of a thief's family:

> God forbid, I should turn hard-hearted, because of their wanting a leg of mutton, in preference to being starved; though they might have no great right to it, according to the forms of law; which, however, is not much impediment to the calls of nature, when a man sees a butcher's stall well covered, and has got nothing within him, except his own poor craving appetite; which is a thing I always take into consideration; though, God forbid, I should protect a thief, no man's property being another's, whether he's poor or rich. (109)

He cannot come to the point, but rambles around it; he is happily unaware of the alternating self-contradictions that reveal his inability to sort out the conflicting demands of compassion and law, and he does not seem to notice that his reasoning has come out on the opposite side from where he actually stands, namely for charity and forgiveness.

Burney attempted in Sir Hugh, as Laurence Sterne did in

Uncle Toby Shandy, to portray a muddle-headed yet irresist-
ibly lovable character; and she did it more convincingly. Her
characterization of Hugh never becomes excessively sentimental, as does that of Toby. She took care to support Hugh's
benevolent feelings with good works, and she called attention
to the limitations of a kind heart undirected by good judgment.
By making Sir Hugh the head of his family, she illustrated the
dangers of a patriarchal system that put power into people's
hands because of birth and sex, rather than ability. Despite his
invariably good intentions, Sir Hugh does considerable dam-
age.

Substantial characterizations like those of Delvile and Sir
Hugh were the products of Burney's mature art, but already
in *Evelina* she was able to hit off characters vividly and use
them to illuminate the problems of women. *Evelina* also
presages weaknesses that were to appear more conspicuously
in her later fiction, inappropriate pathos as well as inappropriate farce. Her sentimental appeals were encouraged by contemporary taste: many of *Evelina*'s admirers were particularly
enthusiastic about the maudlin scene in which Evelina at last
meets her father. Reflecting Burney's ardent devotion to her
own father, this is meant to be the emotional high point of the
novel – Lord Orville never evokes such intensity as Sir John
Belmont. The scene fails, however, because its emotions are
not supported by the plot and characters: Belmont's contrition
and Evelina's love for a father who abused her mother and
whom she has never seen are as false as the rhetoric in which
they are expressed. Similar scenes in the later novels have
been plausibly justified on the grounds that the emotions they
express, over-intense in the terms of the surface narrative, are
appropriate to the grim underlying conditions of women's
lives that are Burney's real subject. In this case at least,
however, no such symbolic point is being made: Burney, like
her readers, enjoyed a good cry and thought weeping was a
sign of virtue.

My objections to the violent emotional effects in *Evelina*, whether farcical or sentimental, are based on my assumption that Burney's aim was to present a lightly satiric view of the world through the eyes of an intelligent, naïve, female observer, who must deal with the normal problems of growing up, problems that are distressing at the time but ultimately manageable. As she herself described it: 'I have only presumed to trace the accidents and adventures to which a "young woman" is liable; I have not pretended to show the world what it actually *is*, but what it *appears* to a girl of seventeen' (*DL* 1:22).

Some recent critics, however, see the grimness of Burney's later vision already existing in *Evelina*. Julia Epstein, in particular, believes that, from the beginning, Burney's anger was central to her creativity. The violent fantasies it produced – nasty practical jokes, accidents and illness, suicide attempted or achieved, nightmares and madness – were effective expressions of the disjunction she saw between the apparent politeness of English society and its habitual violations of women's freedom. Epstein illustrates her interpretation with a jarring passage from Burney's journals, a satire on court etiquette written to her sister Esther in 1785. Frances moves from playful exaggeration – you must not cough or move – to increasing gruesomeness:

> If . . . a black pin runs into your head, you must not take it out. . . . If . . . the agony is very great, you may, privately, bite the inside of your cheek . . . for a little relief; taking care . . . to do it so cautiously as to make no apparent dent outwardly. And, with that precaution, if you even gnaw a piece out, it will not be minded, only be sure . . . to swallow it . . . – for you must not spit. (*DL* 2:353)

Epstein interprets this startling violence as Burney's method for satirizing the cruel strictures of social propriety, particularly as they applied to women. Faced with the need to 'remain

a properly behaved, decorous eighteenth century lady,'
Burney dealt in this way with 'legitimate, and terrorizing,
anger at situations that limit her autonomy' (86–7).

While there is no question about Burney's overflowing
anger, I cannot agree that she mobilized it effectively. It was
too much inhibited by her feelings, especially her love for her
father, to be directed in an artistically effective way. The jokes
that become brutal, the agonies that are disproportionate to
the actual events of her stories, reveal much about Burney's
psychological processes; but they do not make their satiric
points. The sensational elements in *Evelina* – Captain Mirvan's
physical jokes, Evelina's overwrought meetings with her
father, Mr Macartney's near brushes with incest and suicide –
add nothing to the force of Burney's satire and divert attention
from her comic social criticism.

I cannot see evidence of 'simmering rage' in *Evelina*, nor do
I think the heroine's 'predominant emotion' is 'acute anxiety'
(Epstein 4, Staves 368). Burney placed her heroine in situations
that could potentially be dire, but she did not develop that
potentiality. Evelina is frightened when Willoughby gets her
alone in his carriage, but there is no actual danger to her
chastity or even her reputation; he is easily persuaded not to
pursue his advantage, and Lord Orville and the Mirvans, who
might misjudge her, do not. She cannot handle Willoughby in
social repartee, but there is never any doubt that she will successfully resist his sexual schemes. The fact that all threats to
Evelina's essential well-being are dissipated with the same
ease suggests that they never were really serious, however
they might appear to her at the time. It is true that Evelina
endures 'Entrapment and the rising panic it produces,' which
Epstein calls 'the quintessential Burney anxiety' (35). However, unlike Burney's later heroines, she never remains en-
trapped for long. She may be forced into passivity, but she is
not placed in situations where her will is overborne on a
significant question. Although Burney brings grim aspects of

female experience into *Evelina* – Mrs Mirvan's marriage, the race between the old women – these do not touch the heroine. In the world of this book, male brutality can be avoided.[12]

Evelina generally sustains a level of satiric social comedy that was perfectly suited to Burney's theme, the everyday trials of female adolescence, as they appear in relatively superficial social interaction. The effect is very different in *Camilla*, where she dealt with similar material but probed deeply into individual psychology and interaction between people emotionally bound to each other.[13] Burney's later novels were more ambitious than *Evelina*, presenting a more complex and critical view of the world and searching into the problems of human relationships in the family and in society at large. Addressing more serious issues, inviting deeper involvement with the central characters, they moved further from comic romance and therefore required resources beyond those of manners comedy. Instead of pursuing a deeper realism, unfortunately, Burney strove to express her vision through emotional effects that she could not handle effectively – Gothic terror, grotesque farce, harrowing pathos, sublimity. Hence *Evelina* is more artistically effective, though less significant, than her mature novels.

II

CECILIA: A More Probing Look into that World

THE HEROINE OF *Cecilia, or Memoirs of an Heiress*, more mature and self-assured than Evelina and endowed with a comfortable fortune, surely ought to be able to determine the course of her own life – yet her story demonstrates that even a woman who apparently has every resource for independence cannot do so. Cecilia is twenty years old, accustomed to society and experienced enough to have reliable judgment, and hence she is free of 'the timid fears of total inexperience, and . . . the bashful feelings of shame-faced awkwardness' (23) such as inhibit Evelina. With no parents or older relatives living, she has no one whom she feels obligated to obey. Attractive as well as rich, she can marry as she likes, and she does not have to marry anyone. Early in the book, she resolves to take charge of her life and forms a rational plan: she will choose her friends for charm, knowledge, or virtue; devote as much time as she likes to music and reading; and share her superfluous income with carefully chosen, deserving people in need. However, she discovers that she cannot control her destiny any more than Evelina does. Her plan to make the most of her 'affluence, freedom and power' (55) turns out to be bitterly ironic; for in practice she can retain none of them. Affluence gives freedom and power to men, but not to women.

Burney set up her plot to draw attention to the ways in which the institutions of her society devalued and disempowered women. Under the terms of her uncle's will – which when first mentioned seem innocuous and reasonable enough – Cecilia's money will be controlled by three guardians representing a range of qualifications. She will have to live with one of them for the months until she is twenty-one, and she can keep her fortune when she marries only if her husband consents to take her surname. The contrivance of this name clause draws attention to the customary expectation that women give up their names at marriage. The symbolic implications of this sacrifice were recognized even more clearly in the eighteenth century than today, probably because of the greater importance of family and inherited wealth. Richardson's Clarissa opens her list of a woman's losses in marriage: 'To give up her very Name, as a mark of becoming his absolute and dependent property' (1:223).

Because women could not support the family's status by perpetuating its name, they were not considered entitled to their share of the family property. And the possession of money, in Burney's corrupt society as in ours, made one respected and therefore was inextricably connected with feelings of autonomy and self-esteem. Cecilia's predicament in having to choose between fortune and husband is drawn with unusual sharpness, for few women inherited fortunes, and fewer still under conditions that explicitly connected fortune and name; yet it is normal in the sense that any woman who married lost control of her money and thus became in effect 'portionless, tho' an Heiress' (Cutting, 'Defiant Women' 521).

Because the man Cecilia wants to marry is the very one for whom sacrificing his surname would be unthinkable, the apparently insignificant name clause ends up controlling the course of her life. Ironically, she is forced to sacrifice either fortune or happiness for a priority that is meaningless to her. Why should she care whether she bears her uncle's name or her husband's? It is men whose egos are bound up with their surnames – especially when they are distinguished aristocrats like Delvile, but even when they come from prosperous farmer stock like Beverley.

Cecilia is astonished and indignant that Delvile considers his name more important than the love of an ideal wife: 'Well, let him keep his name! since so wonderous its properties, so all-sufficient its preservation, what vanity, what presumption in me, to suppose myself an equivalent for its loss!' (515) Yet, in terms of eighteenth-century attitudes, his distorted valuation was normal. Because of the pride of class and virile self-esteem developed in a patriarchal society, Delvile and his family could only be expected to regard giving up his name for hers as a mean, unmanly concession. Jane West made a great point of the desirability of keeping the family wealth in the family name in her novel *A Tale of the Times* (1799) (C. Johnson 7). She was fanatically conservative, but even so fair-minded a man as Samuel Johnson valued preserving the family name over personal claims; he derided a friend for leaving his property to his sisters in preference to a remote male heir (Boswell, *Life of Johnson* 548). Indeed, I have found few men even today who would cheerfully assume their wife's name at marriage.

Yet, although women were disparaged in the patriarchal family structure, their social identity came from their family. Because Evelina lacks an authorized surname, she does not know 'to whom I most belong' (353). Juliet of *The Wanderer*, without Mr Villars and the social connections he provides, is more completely isolated and devalued for lack of a name: most of the people she meets ignore her personal qualities and good conduct and treat her as a vagabond because she is not attached to a family. And yet, paradoxically, lack of a name gives these women freedom at the same time that it denies them the security of a social niche: 'To lack a name is to belong to no one, that is, to belong to oneself' (Epstein 178). Camilla Tyrold, the only Burney heroine whose name is absolutely normal and unproblematic, is the most restricted of them, the one who can not be conceived of as functioning on her own.

By placing Cecilia under the control of three guardians, not one of them as judicious as she is herself, Burney drew attention to the arbitrary authority imposed on women. Cecilia is blocked at every turn by Mr Harrel, who is grossly irresponsible; Mr Delvile, who is too self-important to care for her; and Mr Briggs, whose only value is money. Eighteenth-century readers would have accepted control of a young woman by her parents as right, but they could recognize the absurdity of control by three obviously incompetent guardians.

This brings into question the patriarchal rationale that women are rightly placed under male guardianship because they cannot function on their own. Theoretically subordinated for their own protection, women actually are more apt to be let down than protected by the men they are forced to depend on, whether they require guidance, like Mrs Harrel, or could in fact manage very well on their own, like Cecilia. Old Mr Delvile, head of his family and a representative of the traditional ruling class, is the very embodiment of patriarchal authority. And yet, far from providing wise guidance and protection, he offers nothing but pompous interference.

As the upper class devalued women because they could not perpetuate their family's status, the middle class devalued them because they could not advance it by making money; for women were debarred from economic opportunities and discouraged from initiative and aggressive self-seeking (Cohn 128). Mr Briggs and Mr Hobson, who assume that making money is the significant exercise of the human intellect, dismiss women as useless and trivial because they were systematically excluded from business. Hobson declares that 'a lady, let her be worth never so much . . . [is] a mere nobody . . . till she can get herself a husband, being she knows nothing of business.' Ladies should not be entrusted with money, because their ignorance of business indicates a general lack of judgment and therefore they are helpless to protect their interests (877–8, 883). By making Hobson a complacent fool, despite the occasional common sense of his remarks, Burney satirizes the man who identifies intelligence with commercial shrewdness.

The main effect of a system in which women are forced to rely on men is the ignoring and devaluation of women. In the very scene where she has finally managed to bring her guardians together so they can conclude mutual business that is essential to her, Cecilia must stand by in helpless silence while four men spend over an hour debating the proper use of riches and the value of aristocratic descent. Only after four male egos have fully expressed themselves can she get anyone to pay attention to her.

One of these egos belongs to the eccentric moralist Mr Albany, a partial exception in this gallery of wrong-headed father figures. Unable to bring herself to pillory virtuous authority, Burney did not clearly develop the comic potential in his high-minded egotism and grandiose concept of himself; but in the settlement scene, she played off Hobson's prosiness against Albany's high-flown preaching to make both look ridiculous. Despite his benevolence, Albany's interaction with Cecilia is controlled by what he expects from her. Regardless of her situation or preoccupations, he interprets her behavior in terms of meeting or failing to meet his demands. If she was not where he thought she would be, he reproaches her for purposely raising his hopes and then disappointing them (746). His language has the familiar ring of the moralist who reviles women for not acting in accordance with his expectations: 'why didst thou fail me? . . . thou thing of fair professions! thou inveigler of esteem! thou vain, delusive promiser of pleasure!' (729) When he bursts in to find her grief-stricken over parting with Delvile, he tells her his own sad story.

Indeed, practically everyone Cecilia meets is too immersed in his or her own concerns to be aware of anyone else's. Old Delvile can see nothing but his own importance, Albany nothing but his charitable missions, fashionable Miss Larolles nothing but the feelings flitting through her head at the moment. As a result, characters keep acting at cross-purposes out of simple unawareness that other people have different aims, as when

Mr Monckton, determined to retain his hold on Cecilia, tries to get her alone at the Harrels', impatiently drags out a general conversation until four of the five other people leave, but cannot get rid of the last obstacle, Mr Morrice. Morrice does not stay by malicious intent: he is merely so eager to ingratiate himself with his betters and so convinced of his ability to do so that he cannot see that Monckton wishes him away (82–4). People are constantly frustrating and irritating one another because they do not care about others enough to be aware of their feelings, even though they compulsively socialize with them.

Because Cecilia is sensitive to other people's feelings and they are oblivious to hers, she is perpetually victimized by their egotism. She is placed in situations where she is urgently impelled to act but is prevented from action by other people immersed in their own trivial preoccupations. As she is rushing to London in order to reach Delvile in time to call off their secret marriage, she is intercepted by Morrice, who insists on riding with her, confident that his company is always welcome. They pass an overturned chaise, and Cecilia, recognizing Miss Larolles's voice, hurries on in order to avoid publicity and delay. But she is forced to wait for the accident victims, because Morrice has taken it upon himself to volunteer her help. They come dawdling up, with no concern in the world except to display their social graces. Larolles's gushing chatter, Captain Aresby's and Mr Meadows's languid affectations, Mr Gosport's need to show off his penetration, Morrice's relentless attempts to ingratiate himself by being obliging are brilliantly accumulated to increase Cecilia's desperate impatience. Even Mrs Charlton, the aged friend whom she has brought along for emotional support, contributes to her exasperation; for the old lady becomes upset by the changes in plan and cannot be hurried (591–613). This scene is more successful than some other long-drawn scenes of suspense in the novel because it is realistic and it integrates comic and serious elements. We can readily empathize with Cecilia's heightening frustration as her urgent business is delayed while other people obliviously do their own thing. The characters' comic turns, which elsewhere may become tediously repetitive, are effective here because they interplay with the heroine's deeply felt emotions.

Burney further illuminates the plight of a serious woman in a world of self-interested fools with her version of the traditional embarrassing disclosure scene. Cecilia has come to visit Henrietta Belfield and is sitting with her in a room that, unknown to her, belongs to Henrietta's brother; she particularly wants to avoid any association with Mr Belfield, since his mother is convinced she is in love with him and Delvile's hostile father is eagerly seizing on these rumors in order to discredit her. Cecilia finds herself trapped when Mrs Belfield enters the outer room, since she would interpret Cecilia's presence as confirmation of her love for Belfield. Then old Delvile arrives to confirm the rumors, and Cecilia must sit and listen to Mrs Belfield misrepresent her motives, lest she confirm his suspicions by appearing. She and Henrietta manage to keep Belfield quiet when he unexpectedly returns to his room. But then a meddlesome neighbor drops in and asks about the two sedan chairs in the entry. Mrs Belfield realizes there must be a visitor in the inner room and throws open the door to discover Cecilia with her son, thereby apparently confirming her own and old Delvile's belief that they are involved in a secret love-affair.

The situation recalls the similar embarrassments of Tom Jones and Joseph Surface (*Tom Jones* 14:2, the screen scene in *The School for Scandal*). The difference is that both the male characters deserve their discomfort. Cecilia, through no fault of her own, is 'abashed, perplexed, and embarrassed' (785). She is constantly being kept from doing what is important to her because of other people's demands or wrongly judged because of the positions into which other people force her. Her enforced passivity is suggested even by the chapter headings. Every one of them is a noun, usually an abstract one: 'A Supplication,' 'A Provocation,' 'A Debate,' and finally 'A Termination.'

With beauty and money, Cecilia's problem is to fend off suitors; Burney makes clear that this gives her no more freedom than the woman who is trying to find a suitable husband. People are constantly pressuring her to marry them or their protégés and ignoring her distaste and denials. Her trusted friend Mr Monckton plans to marry her when his old wife dies, and 'had long looked upon her as his future property' (9); and Captain Aresby is annoyed when another man sits next to her at a party because he regarded her 'as his natural property for the morning' (13). Although Sir Robert Floyer has no other distinction than his 'expression of invincible assurance,' he expects to marry Cecilia simply because he wishes to do so; from their first meeting he looks her over as 'property he means to cheapen' (34), and he is aggrieved when she does not comply with his plans. Whenever they are together – a common event that she cannot avoid, although she thoroughly dislikes him – he fixes her with a bold stare, while she can only avert her eyes in embarrassment; thus he successfully reduces her to 'an object to be gazed at' (37). Even young Delvile at first 'seemed to think her the undoubted property of the baronet' (302).

The men's persistence in believing that Cecilia will marry Floyer, despite her repeated, decisive refusals, is carried beyond literal probability. However, Harrel's dismissal of her feelings truly expresses the ease with which a dominant group can disregard the wishes of a subordinate one:

> I never saw in Miss Beverley any disapprobation beyond what it is customary for young ladies of a sentimental turn to shew; and every body knows that where a gentleman is allowed to pay his devoirs for any length of time, no lady intends to use him very severely. (367–8)

Women were inhibited from protesting forcefully against other people's plans, and their failure to do so was interpreted as acquiescence. The worldly-wise Monckton explains Harrel's reasoning:

> So many of your sex have been subdued by perseverance, and so many have been conquered by boldness, that he supposed when he united two such powerful besiegers in the person of a baronet, he should vanquish all obstacles. By assuring you that the world thought the marriage already settled, he hoped to surprise you into believing there was no help for it, and by the suddenness and vehemence of the attack, to frighten and hurry you into compliance. His own wife, he knew, might have been managed thus with ease, and so, probably, might his sister, and his mother, and his cousin. (370)

How cunningly Monckton analyzes the way people can be pressured without actual coercion: without violating a woman's legal rights, without incurring the guilt of forcing her to do anything she explicitly declared against, men could nevertheless impose their will. They could take advantage of her socialized inability to assert herself to bully her into compliance, and then interpret her yielding to confirm the assumption that she is naturally passive. Having trained her to give up her wishes out of feminine gentleness, they take her doing so as evidence that her wishes could not have been important even to herself.

Dr John Gregory, author of *A Father's Legacy to His Daughters* (1774), a widely read and respected conduct manual for young women, was a well-intentioned and kindly father; yet his attitude toward female self-determination was much like Harrel's. He saw nothing wrong with a situation in which 'what is commonly called love' among women 'is rather gratitude, and a partiality to the man who prefers' them to the rest of their sex, so that women often marry men 'with little of either personal esteem or affection.' He calmly explains that it is unlikely that a woman of sense and taste will find many men she can esteem, more unlikely that one of those few will care for her, still less likely that that one will be her first choice. However, he cheerfully assures women that this is no hardship: 'As, therefore, Nature has not given you that unlimited range in your choice which we enjoy, she has wisely and benevolently assigned to you a greater flexibility of taste on the subject' (80–3). *Cecilia* and other women's novels performed an important service for women in presenting model heroine after model heroine who has firm, decided opinions on what she wants in a husband.

Because women's wishes were considered unimportant, it was not necessary to listen to them. Over and over, Cecilia earnestly tries to make a point to some man; and he discounts every word she says. Her positions are rationally thought out and she is absolutely truthful and straightforward, and yet people will not believe her. Guardian Briggs has resolved to marry her to 'a good and careful husband' who can manage her money, and guardian Delvile, to an inane young lord – and neither can hear that she is in no hurry to marry and that she wishes to choose a husband for his personal qualifications. Even young Delvile disregards Cecilia's own testimony as he assumes the stereotyped view that a woman who takes any interest in a young man must be in love with him:

> . . . he, half gayly, half reproachfully, said, 'Whence is it that young ladies, even such whose principles are most strict, seem universally, in those affairs where their affections are concerned, to think hypocrisy necessary, and deceit amiable? and hold it graceful to disavow to-day, what they may perhaps mean publicly to acknowledge to-morrow?' (183)

The nightmare journey through London streets at the end of the book, in which Cecilia's repeated failures to make people listen to her finally drive her into delirium, symbolically exaggerates this situation. In her madness, she cries out, 'I am married, and no one will listen to me!' (903). Young women might think that, since marriage supposedly marked maturity in women, it would give them the status of responsible adults; actually, they were no more respectfully listened to than they had been as girls.[14]

Burney could have drawn these elements of Cecilia's story from her own personal experience, for she too had suffered from the assumptions that a woman had better be married off as soon as possible and that her preferences were insignificant and her professions not to be believed. When she was almost twenty-three, she went to a dull family tea party and met Thomas Barlow, who lodged with her grandmother's friend. He was an inoffensive young man, but Burney did not find him at all interesting or attractive. She rebuffed him when he tried to engage her in serious conversation and was amazed when he sent her a letter proposing marriage. Her first impulse was to reject it out of hand, but then she reflected that she was not 'an independent member of society' and mentioned it to her father (*ED* 2:50). He alarmed her by telling her to reserve her answer. Her silence encouraged Barlow to send her a second letter.

Meanwhile, her grandmother, maiden aunts and sister Esther urged her to accept him. Even worse, Crisp – a man whose right-thinking and right-feeling she particularly trusted – wrote to warn her against rejecting a respectable well-to-do man, because such another might very well never come along. It seemed that the whole family was uniting to force her to spend her life with a man she could not possibly care for. Her last hope was her father, who had not yet spoken. If he urged her, she knew she could not resist. She was pathetically grateful when he told her she could live with him as long as she liked (*ED* 2:47–70). It is chilling to think that a well-intentioned family, with Frances's interests genuinely at heart, could press her toward an unwanted marriage in the manner of the sinister Harlowes in *Clarissa*; and that they all felt that her preference, admiration or liking were not important enough to be reckoned with. Marriage was typically the most important

choice a woman made, the one which defined her circumstances for the rest of her life. And yet she was supposed to
accept passively whoever presented himself and was acceptable to her family – as if she did not care or her wishes did not
count.

Barlow's courtship, superficially gallant and affectionate,
betrays his lack of interest in her feelings: he keeps assuring
her that he knows she will make him happy and even tells her
that her refusal 'is more pleasing than any other lady's acceptance' (*ED* 2:67–8). His bland insistence that she would accept
him despite her repeated rejections provides a precedent in
real life for Harrel's assumption that women's resolutions
could always be overwhelmed by male persistence. Burney
and Cecilia were unusual in their refusal to yield to this
pressure; in actual life, most women, in the absence of other
possibilities, would have been unwilling or unable to hold out
for 'Social Simpathy of character & taste' (*JL* 3:9).

Cecilia's enforced passivity is most vividly dramatized at the
Harrels' masquerade. Terry Castle, noting that Cecilia spends
this scene as the center of attention, courted by many men,
argues that it is her moment of triumph (270).[15] Burney,
however, like most of her intelligent female contemporaries,
understood that such tributes were usually empty and that
gallantry can be used to claim ownership. In their every en-
counter in *Evelina*, Sir Clement Willougby professes chivalric
devotion to the heroine while overbearing her wishes. The
masquerade scene demonstrates the ironic contrast between
the apparent privilege and respect that were accorded women
– and eighteenth-century gentlemen sincerely believed that
women in England enjoyed higher esteem than anywhere else
– and their actual powerlessness.

Because Cecilia, like Burney herself, enjoys a novel experience, she looks forward to the masquerade and finds some
pleasure in it, principally from its absurdity – but her freedom
to observe is soon lost, as she finds herself besieged by masked

men, from whom she cannot escape. She is soon approached by a devil (Monckton), who bows to her profoundly but blocks her attempt to move away, so that, 'preferring captivity to resistance, she was again obliged to seat herself' (107). Driven off temporarily by a Don Quixote (Belfield), whose chivalric homage is so extreme as to function as parody, the devil returns to Cecilia and keeps 'his prey to himself' by growling. In terms of the literal situation, it is never clear why she cannot break free from him; but, if the scene is taken as representative of women's general predicament, it dramatizes the dilemma of women who must either give up their wishes or violate their own notions of feminine decorum by being unpleasingly forceful.

Finally a white domino (young Delvile) gets rid of the devil, but he points the moral by telling her many men 'would be happy to confine you in the same manner.' The devil returns again, and, it seems, the only way he can be kept at bay is by Cecilia's letting herself be guarded (and immobilized) by three other men, who surround her chair. Even so, the devil easily pushes his way past and lies down before her – another image of apparent respect and real domination. The fact that even Delvile does not effectively rescue her suggests that there is no escape for ladies within the chivalric context that objectifies them under a pretence of gallant respect: 'She was made an object of general attention, yet could neither speak nor be spoken to' (111–12). Only vulgar Briggs, who has no concept of chivalry, can get rid of the devil; then he in turn imposes himself on her.

Cecilia is rendered even more conspicuous and vulnerable by being in ordinary dress. Everyone watches her, and she alone is unprotected by the disguises that release others from the normal constraints of their social roles.[16] The masquerading men can express their inner natures and feelings as they like without being held to account, because they are not recognized. Even the benign man, young Delvile, knows all about Cecilia while she does not even know who he is. Her situation represents that of young women in general, who had to make their way in a perilous world without adequate information; their relative inexperience and inability to control events made it difficult for them to evaluate others, and yet it was essential to their well-being to do so. At the same time, they had to worry about others evaluating them on the basis of appearance. Since reputation was more important to them than to men, and more dependent on general public opinion, they must have felt themselves uncomfortably under constant scrutiny.

Cecilia is a thoughtful young woman in a society of egotistical fools. She, and her omniscient narrator, critically examine the world as the *ingénue* Evelina could not. And their criticism is devastating. Despite her demure manner, Burney judged fools mercilessly and detested socializing with them. When Crisp suspected her of overdrawing a character in her journal, she assured him of its strict factuality:

> . . . the world, and especially the Great world, is so filled with absurdity of various sorts, now bursting forth in impertinence, now in pomposity, now giggling in silliness, and now yawning in dulness, that there is no occasion for invention to draw what is striking in every possible species of the ridiculous. (*DL* 1:312)

Cecilia, introduced into the most fashionable London society, meets a rich variety of such people and constantly finds herself in 'large parties . . . collected . . . without any possible reason why they might not as well be separated' (27). This select society lacks brains, heart, and even politeness; not only do married couples care nothing for each other, but they see nothing wrong with such indifference. Cecilia resolves 'to drop all idle and uninteresting acquaintance, who while they contribute neither to use nor pleasure, make so large a part of the community, that they may properly be called the underminers of existence' (55). But once she has got her own home and can do so, she finds that excluding 'the useless or frivolous' from her house would mean 'driving from her half her acquaintance,' that confining herself to 'the society of the wise, good, and intelligent' would leave her isolated (792–3).

Cecilia persistently tries to direct her life by her own reason in this absurd world. Burney pointedly contrasts her right judgment and rational self-control with the folly and self-indulgence of the more powerful people around her. Cecilia is astounded by Harrel's treatment of the carpenter Hill for its irrationality even more than for its inhumanity: 'that he could take pride in works which not even money had made his own, and live with undiminished splendour, when his credit itself began to fail, seemed to her incongruities so irrational, that hitherto she had supposed them impossible' (85). Although feminine softness and her obliging disposition have induced her to comply with the Harrels' senseless extravagance, she is finally provoked to consult 'nothing but reason and principle' (101). When at last she gets control of her own money, she arranges her household according to a perfect golden mean, which she arrives at by independent thinking: 'The system of her economy . . . was formed by rules of reason, and her own ideas of right, and not by compliance with example' (792). Her initial resistance to her love for Delvile is motivated by reason rather than the conventional maidenly modesty: 'as her passions were under the controul of her reason . . . she started at her danger the moment she perceived it, and instantly determined to give no weak encouragement to a prepossession which neither time nor intimacy had justified' (251). When he comes to her frantic, thinking he has fatally wounded Monckton in a duel, she realizes that 'To censure him . . . would both be cruel and vain; yet to pretend she was satisfied with his conduct, would be doing violence to her judgment and veracity' (845).

It is ironic that this exemplar of rational morality is forced by her uncle's will to live with the Harrels and forced by the

Harrels into constant empty socializing, and further constrained by the general pressure on women to conform and comply with the people around them. Women, especially young ones, were not only trapped in social circumstances, but blamed as unwomanly if they criticized or tried to change them. The irony deepens when Albany scolds Cecilia for associating with a dissipated crowd. He blames her for failing to meet his abstract standards of right, even though, as a woman, she has to live not by reason but by the wishes of those around her and by the unreasonable conventions governing proper female behavior. Women were pressed into appearing frivolous and silly and then blamed for it.

Burney insisted on her heroine's rationality not only as a protest against social constraints, but as a refutation of the antifeminist charges that woman is a prey to her feelings or a mere sexual object. Even conservative eighteenth-century women writers concurred with Wollstonecraft in exhorting their sex to be 'rational creatures' (*Vindication* 81). Wollstonecraft based her argument for women's rights on the rational capacity they share with men, and even women who thought she carried her arguments too far agreed that women are plunged into 'meannesses, cares, and sorrows . . . by the prevailing opinion, that they were created rather to feel than reason, and that all the power they obtain, must be obtained by their charms and weakness.' For this makes them 'entirely dependent . . . on man, not only for protection, but advice'; it makes a woman 'rely for all her happiness on a being subject to like infirmities with herself.' This leads them, like Burney's brainless Indiana in *Camilla*, to cling to a man 'In the most trifling danger . . . with parasitical tenacity, piteously demanding succour,' so 'their *natural* protector extends his arm, or lifts up his voice, to guard the lovely trembler – from what? Perhaps the frown of an old cow' (111, 153; Burney even borrowed Wollstonecraft's example in Book 2, Chapters 10, 11).

A Vindication of the Rights of Woman (1792) disparages sexual love, on the grounds that it makes women dependent, blinds them to their true interests and betrays a lack of rational control. Many women preferred friendship and esteem, which implied women's ability to value mental and moral excellence and men's recognition of these qualities in women.[17] Without rational self-control, a woman was helplessly dependent on men, who might seduce her or dangle her in suspense while they considered whether to marry her. Rationality was the route to self-respect and such freedom as was available to women. On the other hand, as Wollstonecraft and Cecilia were both to discover, freedom achieved by avoiding emotional dependence was achieved at the cost of ruthlessly repressing their own feelings. In this way, paradoxically, the rational ideal could restrict as well as liberate them.

In the first part of *Cecilia*, the heroine's rational course of conduct is impeded only by other people's folly or prejudice; in the second part, it is undermined by her own love for Delvile and his mother. Cecilia's ambition to be always controlled by reason proves to be as illusory as her intention of living her life by a rational plan. She falls in love with Delvile and realizes that her happiness is 'no longer in her own power.' Even though 'the choice of her heart' is 'confirmed by her judgment' (252), she is apprehensive more than elated. She is deeply mortified when Delvile accidentally discovers that she loves him, because he now knows himself 'the master of her destiny' (551).

How much greater is her mortification when she discovers that she is emotionally dependent on a man who hesitates to marry her. He balks at giving up his name – an obstacle that represents all the degrading criteria that qualified or disqualified women for marriage. Loving marriage was idealized by the later eighteenth century, yet wives were not selected for the mental and moral qualities that would make them affectionate, congenial companions, but for birth, money and physical beauty. Because of men's misplaced priorities, deserving women were disparaged in the all-important marriage market for deficiencies that should have been irrelevant and were entirely out of their control.

Cecilia's sense of her merits is just, but she is perhaps a little complacent, certainly naïve, in assuming that Delvile and his family will be delighted to welcome her as his wife, disregarding the problem of the required name change. At first she is rather pleased that he does not propose, because this will give her more opportunity to investigate his worth. Burney pokes gentle fun at the 'happy intellectual arrangement' by which Cecilia accounts for Delvile's silence and the scenario she develops in which she will mingle 'dignity with the frankness with which she meant to receive his addresses' (253, 310).

She is confident that she controls the situation, until she has to watch her lover go off to consider whether she is worth giving up his name for. He will decide whether they are to marry and then 'acquaint her with his decree, not doubting her concurrence which ever way he resolved' (552). She is forced to recognize the difference in status between the most deserving woman and the male heir to an eminent family. Delvile is exercising the prerogative of Lord Orville and other romance heroes, but here Burney remarks and resents the humiliation that this imposes upon the subject of his choice. When he finally does propose, Cecilia does not feel happiness, but anxiety, humiliation and guilt. She lets him pressure her into a secret marriage, which implies that she is not worthy of being accepted by his family, and immediately regrets her decision. She vacillates until she sinks into a state where she cannot act effectively at all.

At this point, Cecilia's situation is complicated by guilt connected with Mrs Delvile. She is the only authority figure in the book who has an emotional hold over Cecilia, because Cecilia loves and respects her. Having exorcized the overpowering father figure by reducing the male authorities to absurdity and impotence, Burney replaces him with a mother. Unlike her husband, Mrs Delvile has natural qualities to support her social distinction. Her arrogance has a basis in genuine superiority. She can be amused by Briggs's brazen intrusion into their home, which provokes her husband to sputtering outrage. She can appreciate Cecilia, whereas most of the men see her simply as a pretty young thing who may as well be, who will not even mind being, married off to any man who seems suitable. Mrs Delvile is amenable to rational persuasion and will ultimately come to approve her son's marriage to Cecilia. Burney makes clear the painful inequity of Mrs Delvile's position, forced by her own moral principles as well as the law to obey a man she cannot honor, and does not criticize her clear-sighted perception of her husband's weaknesses nor her ingenious evasion of their consequences.

Yet, by initially opposing the marriage that will make her son and her friend happy, Mrs Delvile promotes the very system that has victimized her. Married by her family to a man she cannot respect or love, she has ruthlessly curbed her acute feelings and strong passions 'by reason and principle'; despite her misery, she 'steadily behaved to him with the strictest propriety' (461). Having sacrificed her own inclinations to convention, she is convinced that the most odious of all things in a woman is 'a daring defiance of the world and its opinions' (498). Her pride forces her to identify with the values for which she has sacrificed her happiness and to give her life meaning by forcing her son to carry on the family name. Her obsession with the patriarchal name emphasizes that these values are alien to her own interests as a woman.

Therefore, her genuine love for Cecilia and belief that she would be right for Mortimer do not prompt her to question her principles, but merely to argue that her own sacrifice of feeling should set an example for the younger woman: 'In tearing you from my son, I partake all the wretchedness I give, but your own sense of duty must something plead for the strictness with which I act up to mine' (641). Thus the tradition of female self-sacrifice is carried from the older (and more powerful) generation to the younger. The masochistic rationale for this feminine morality comes out in Mrs Delvile's letter urging Cecilia to renounce Mortimer in person: 'we came not hither to enjoy, but to suffer; and happy only are those whose sufferings have neither by folly been sought, nor by guilt been merited' (668). People of a subject class, obliged to sacrifice their will to others', make a moral merit of sacrifice to shore up their self-respect; thus their very pride may spur them to self-subjection. Hester Thrale recognized her own rigorously self-sacrificing mother in Mrs Delvile and declared that her mother would have behaved in the same way (*DL* 2:83, 126).

Mrs Delvile feels justified in expecting Cecilia to make the same sacrifice of personal feeling to principle that she has herself made. Cecilia can remain mentally independent of her inadequate male mentors, despite outward frustrations; but she finds it intolerably painful to resist the admirable parent, Mrs Delvile. She regrets consenting to a secret marriage because she dreads offending Mrs Delvile and disappointing her expectations of 'even exemplary virtue' (577). She is angry, for she is intellectually convinced that the family should be happy to receive her; but she has to yield to this woman because she loves and admires her. She cannot resist Mrs Delvile's offer of a higher esteem than one human being ever felt for another,' nor her appeal to the rationality on which Cecilia prides herself: 'Who is there like you? . . . So open to reason, so ingenuous in error! so rational! so just! so feeling, yet so wise!' (638, 651)

Mrs Delvile is misusing reason by identifying it with repression of feelings inconvenient to the dominant class, as some senior characters in *Camilla* were to do. Burney's attitude in *Camilla* is ambiguous, but in the climactic scene where Mrs Delvile confronts her son and Cecilia to force them to give each other up, there is no question of the author's condemnation. At the very time that Mrs Delvile is exhorting Cecilia and her

Cecilia

son to follow reason by renouncing each other, she is yielding increasingly to passion. Immediately after she has rebuked Mortimer for arguing reasonably that he should marry Cecilia, she collapses in a stroke – the extreme opposite of maintaining rational control (679–80). Actually, Mortimer too indulges in selfish passion, even though he advocates the reasonable view. As usual, Cecilia is the rational, self-controlled victim of other people's violence and egotism.

Contemporary readers were disturbed by the characteriza-tion of Mrs Delvile, finding a contradiction between her admir-able qualities and her rigor toward the heroine. Crisp objected that her violent behavior in the confrontation scene was out of character. The scene is certainly overwrought, filled with fainting on Cecilia's part and rant on the Delviles'; and it is superfluous, since Cecilia has already given Delvile up because of the interruption in their attempted secret marriage. Yet it was curiously important to Burney, who wrote to Crisp:

> The conflict scene for Cecilia, between the mother and son . . . is the very scene for which I wrote the whole book, and so entirely does my plan hang upon it, that I must abide by its reception in the world, or put the whole thing behind the fire. (DL 2:71)

Crisp's dissatisfaction is understandable. Despite Burney's insistence that she had shown in Mrs Delvile from the begin-ning 'how the greatest virtues and excellences may be totally obscured by the indulgence of violent passions and the ascend-ancy of favourite prejudices,' she in fact presented no evidence of 'violence and obduracy' (DL 2:72, 73) until Mrs Delvile became Cecilia's antagonist. Far from being habitually violent, Mrs Delvile is praised for controlling her passions. Up to this point, Burney palliates her pride by telling us it is based on gen-uine intrinsic superiority and directed at fools such as Cecilia herself finds tiresome; the only difference is that Mrs Delvile is in a position to select her society. It is only when the pride is opposed to Cecilia's interests that it becomes censurable. The wavering judgment suggests that Burney was identifying with Mrs Delvile's victim, sharing her hurt and resentment when her friend turns into her opponent.

Actually, the climactic confrontation was less 'between the mother and son' than between mother and daughter. As such, it tapped into Burney's deepest emotions and conflicts. This is the only scene in her fiction where the heroine is unequivocally opposed and let down by a revered authority figure. The opposition itself is distressing, but the disillusionment is even more so. Instead of supporting Cecilia's interests, this parental friend is pursuing her own interests at Cecilia's expense. Instead of serving as a model, she is promoting the distorted values and narrow conventionality that Cecilia must resist. She misuses her influence to force Cecilia to act against her own feelings and her own sense of right. Mrs Delvile particularly betrays her own sex, as she pressures Cecilia to sacrifice her happiness to masculine values. Yet she may also be standing in for Burney's father, manifesting his false values and selfishness, but in the doubly indirect form of a mother surrogate rather than a father. The most intense and problematic relationship in *Cecilia*, as in Burney's life, was with a beloved parent.

Even after Mrs Delvile removes the significant obstacle by consenting to a marriage in which Delvile will keep his name at the expense of Cecilia's fortune, the wedding is strangely flat. Cecilia feels only apprehension during the ceremony, and there is no mention of joy or love (831). The troubled course of her relationship with the man she loves is more suggestive of doubts about the marriage that culminates it than of obstacles happily overcome. The final paragraph of the novel, as Castle points out, is remarkably negative, considering that Cecilia has attained her goal: namely, marriage to Delvile without losing the friendship of his mother. The emphasis is not on happy fulfillment but on limitation: although she has plenty of money, she sometimes murmurs at being 'portionless, tho' an

HEIRESS'; she reflects that no one has happiness 'without some misery' and, in the closing words of the novel, bears 'partial evil with chearfullest resignation' (941). Although she has married the man of her dreams, her marriage brings loss and limitation, to which she must resign herself. And yet the only loss specifically mentioned is that of her fortune, which is not really important. The family has plenty to live comfortably, and Burney felt that congeniality was the only thing essential in marriage (*JL* 3:9).

Nevertheless, it is clear that Cecilia has, in Millamant's words, dwindled into a wife. Castle perhaps overstates when she sees Cecilia as a 'revolutionary individual' forced to give up 'joy, liberty, the dream of being remarkable' by a repressive society (284); but Cecilia has undoubtedly lost the heiress's independence and self-esteem. Although she would in any case have lost control of her fortune on marriage, her formal relinquishment reinforces the point that a woman could not have the emotional fulfillment of marriage without giving up the ego fulfillment made possible by financial independence.[18] Burney passionately defended her mixed ending against the protests of readers like Edmund Burke, who would have preferred clear-cut happiness or misery. The importance she attached to it – and perhaps her contemporaries' discomfort with it – results from what she was saying indirectly.

Burney had always been impressed by what women give up in marriage. As an adolescent, viewing a wedding between two people she did not know, she had been moved to comment, 'O how short a time does it take to put an eternal end to a woman's liberty!' (*ED* 1:17) A conscientious woman felt herself obligated to subordinate her aspirations to her husband's; the most considerate lover would turn into a husband conscious of his right to command. On one occasion between her aborted and her real marriage, Cecilia admits Delvile because she sees the incongruity of turning from her door 'a man who, but for an incident the most incomprehensible, would now have been the sole master of herself and her actions' (655). Burney, who had acceptable alternatives as Cecilia did, doubted that she could be happier married than single. Considering the unlikelihood of finding a truly congenial man – she had not yet experienced romantic love – she did not think the risk worth while: 'I had never made any vow against Marriage, but I had LONG – LONG been firmly persuaded it was – *for* ME – a state of too much hazard, & too little promise, to draw me from my individual plans & purposes' (*JL* 3:9).

In *Cecilia*, Burney was challenging a fundamental assumption of romantic fiction and of the actual life that fiction idealized. Escaping an unsuitable marriage or surmounting obstacles to achieve a good one were common problems in eighteenth-century women's novels. Unhappy wives often appear as secondary characters, but the heroine is distinguished by being given the opportunity to make an ideal marriage, which will bring her the total fulfillment that marriage was supposed to bring. Here, however, Burney suggests that even the best of marriages diminishes a woman by subjecting her to a man.

Through most of her trials, Cecilia remains a comic heroine. Burney subjects her to difficulties that are exasperating, mortifying, sometimes painful, but ultimately manageable and relieved by a humorous discernment of mistakes and cross-purposes; hence she can view Cecilia with detachment and occasional light mockery. After she has given up Delvile, she has a dream of a life of independent philanthropy, which recalls the rational plan of her early days but places a stronger emphasis on good works. Her dream expresses benevolence, idealism – and a touch of grandiosity. Instead of traditional feminine good works, she will perform heroic ones traditionally appropriated by male philanthropists:

> In her sleep she bestowed riches, and poured plenty upon the land; she humbled the oppressor, she exalted the oppressed; slaves were raised to dignities, captives restored to liberty; beggars saw smiling abundance, and wretchedness was

banished the world. From a cloud in which she was supported
by angels, Cecilia beheld these wonders. . . . (711)

Doody points to echoes of the mission of Aeneas and Rome,
as expressed in Dryden's translation of *The Aeneid*, which
emphasize the ironic contrast between Cecilia's view of an
heiress as a benefactor of society and the world's view of an
heiress as 'an object to be taken' (intro. to *Cecilia* xxxiv). But
the passage also recalls Johnson's *Rasselas*, daydreaming in
his Happy Valley of correcting the ills of society (ch. 4). Both
young people are impractical as well as amiable, imagining
themselves gloriously rising to challenges that will never come
to them. In her benevolent egotism, Cecilia also sees herself
as her saintly namesake, as apotheosized in continental paint-
ings; thus she would be a worshiped female saint as well as
an active male hero.

But by the time Cecilia has married Delvile, and still has
trials to undergo, Burney has lost her esthetic distance from
her heroine; and comedy turns into pathetic melodrama. Misfortunes pile up toward the end of the book, as if the story
were headed for a tragic ending. Cecilia's parting from her
dependents when ejected from her home, her distraction
when unable to find her husband, her resultant imprisonment
as a madwoman and near approach to death, the procession
of remorseful mourners by her bed, all recall Clarissa's experiences – with the significant difference that Clarissa really was
a tragic victim. Cecilia's self-respect was never assaulted as
Clarissa's was by the rape, and therefore her madness and
brain-fever are not external expressions of inner agony, but contrived melodramatic effects.[19] Cecilia will not die, but instead
will live quite happily with the man she loves and his family;
and therefore Albany's funeral elegy over her is factitious.

It is true that these events have an exaggerated symbolic
truth. Castle points out that Cecilia the heiress and independent human being does die (276–7); and Straub suggests that

Burney uses Cecilia's madness to let her express anger and resistance to marriage that she never could express as a decorous sane woman, as when in delirium she exclaims that Delvile will 'mangle and destroy' her and mistakes him for the villain, Monckton (906; Straub 175–6). The interpretations are plausible, but Burney could have made her points more effectively by developing them in realistic narrative. I suspect that she aimed for simple emotional, rather than symbolic, effects in these scenes. Eighteenth-century readers enjoyed weeping over the apparent dying of a blameless young woman. It was these distressful scenes that drew most admiration, even from sophisticated readers like Thrale. Although she enjoyed the comic parts, she particularly looked forward to crying herself 'blind over the conclusion' of *Cecilia*; ''tis so excessively pathetic' (*DL* 2:53–4).

III

CAMILLA: Family Relationships Complicating Entrance into the World

LIKE EVELINA, Camilla Tyrold is an adolescent, entering the world at the age of seventeen. Her inexperience leads her to make constant mistakes, and she is praised for her 'modest confusion' when she is brought into the center of a group (474). However, Burney did not present *Camilla* as a novel – that is, a mere love-story – but as 'sketches of Characters & morals, put in action' (*JL* 3:117). She promised a more serious moral purpose and greater psychological complexity, with particular emphasis on the difficulty of understanding other people's hearts or even our own (7). In accordance with this weightier aim, *Camilla* is more realistic than *Evelina*. In every way, it reverses the wish-fulfilling fantasies of the earlier book. Evelina is free of family entanglements because of romantic complications such as unacknowledged marriage and interchanged infants; Camilla is in the much more ordinary situation of having a complete family – who, being an eighteenth-century family, constrain her actions. The Tyrold daughters are adoring and subordinate, while Mr Villars centers his life on his foster-daughter and declares that to serve her he 'would with transport die!' (20) His authority is wholly benign and helpful, consisting only of giving Evelina the guidance she needs to achieve happy fulfillment. Parental authority works exactly the way it should – and with a perfection rarely found in actual life.

Inexperienced and separated from home, Evelina makes only minor mistakes, for which she is quickly excused. Burney set up Camilla's story so as to throw her into situations where she can hardly avoid making serious mistakes, and she is rigorously judged for every one of them – sometimes by authority figures who are wise and good, but never available to help her; sometimes by her own superego, which they have formed. Evelina cannot face introducing her unpresentable family to Sir Clement and foolishly goes off with him alone in his carriage; this error produces some unpleasant anxious minutes, but he refrains from assaulting her and Lord Orville does not misjudge her. Camilla cannot manage her money prudently, and sends her father to debtors' prison. Lord Orville combines impressive excellence with gentle diffidence and constant consideration of Evelina's needs; he is ever ready to offer helpful advice, but never censorious or domineering. Edgar Mandlebert is a much more realistic conception: his excellence brings with it self-righteousness and exacting standards; his wise advice, a disabling imposition of superiority; his concern for Camilla's welfare, exigent requirements on her. *Evelina* leaves us with a serene confidence that the heroine's problems have been resolved; *Camilla* leaves us with a depressed apprehension that the heroine can only be protected from life's insoluble problems by timidity and caution.

In developing the two major relationships in *Camilla*, those of the heroine with her lover and with her parents, Burney drew more directly on her deepest feelings than she did in her other novels. The result is more emotional intensity and psychological complexity, but a less clear vision. After writing *Cecilia*, Burney had two humiliating romantic relationships. First the Reverend George Owen Cambridge and later Colonel Stephen Digby (called Mr Fairly in her journals) paid her prolonged and marked attention, acted like suitors, but never proposed. These experiences strongly impressed upon her the power of men to bestow or withhold marriage and the extent to which high-principled men can blandly exploit women. Although the experiences were too painful and embarrassing to be directly transmitted into fiction, they are reflected in

Edgar's protracted hesitations about proposing and in Camilla's anxious speculations about whether he loves her and whether she has somehow displeased him.[20]

The connection between Mr Tyrold and Dr Burney is more direct. Camilla's adoration of her father and compelling need to please him mirror Burney's feelings for hers. Paternal approval was of overwhelming importance to both of them: 'Elevated by the kindness of a father so adored, to deserve his good opinion now included every wish' (345). Thus both fathers could control their daughters through gentle affection rather than severity and reproof. As Camilla will not disturb her father by telling him about her debts, Dr Burney's whole family concealed dissensions from him. Frances wrote to Thrale: 'Surely we should profit little from the example he has himself set us of patience & sweetness at *all* Times, to prefer our own convenience to his *dearest tranquillity*' (qtd Hemlow 40). Developing the relationship between the heroine and her beloved father involved Burney's most intense feelings, which, as projected on Camilla, become almost pathological. Fleeing on a visit to avoid confronting her mother over her debts, she flew into her father's arms, 'rather agonised than affectionate; kissed his hands with fervour, kissed every separate finger . . . caught and pressed to her lips even the flaps of his coat, and scarce restrained herself from bending to kiss his feet' (792).

Camilla's dependence upon the respected authorities who surround her reflects Burney's own problem with self-assertion. She had a keen ear for pomposity and a keen resentment of bullying, but she could not resist or even clearly formulate resentment against authority that she regarded as just. To some extent, this was a problem for girls in general. Virtuous children were expected to respect, as well as obey, their parents; and girls were expected to be more willingly submissive than boys and assumed to be less capable of making their own decisions. Contrast, for example, the respectful firmness with which the paragon Sir Charles Grandison handles his unworthy father and the servitude that the paragon Clarissa submits to from hers. (Clarissa does consider the possibility of resistance – "'tis only "being the less beloved"'' [1:33, 48] – but, like Burney, finds it almost impossible to put her insight into practice.) A virtuous young woman could not take action regardless of her parents unless pressed to extremity like Clarissa, and even Clarissa must be punished.

Typically, eighteenth-century women novelists avoided the problem of parental authority by making their heroine an orphan. (As Claudia Johnson has pointed out, ultraconservative novelists like Hannah More and Jane West made a point of giving their heroines families in order to demonstrate their allegiance to hierarchical rule [84].) Only an orphan could move the plot by her own decisions without incurring a charge of disobedient wilfulness. This was the case of Charlotte Lennox's Arabella, Elizabeth Inchbald's Miss Milner (*A Simple Story*, 1791) and Charlotte Smith's Monimia (*The Old Manor House*, 1793). Orlando, Smith's hero, has a family – but, being a young man, he is entitled to use his own judgment anyway. He is a dutiful and considerate son, mindful of his obligations to his mother and sisters, but himself decides what these are, as does Burney's Mortimer Delvile. The orphaned state that signified forlorn isolation to nineteenth-century heroes signified freedom for eighteenth-century heroines. Burney herself used this convention in three of her novels, as Cecilia and the Wanderer Juliet are actual orphans, and Evelina one in effect.

In *Camilla*, however, she faced the problem of growing up under parental authority. It is significant that she sketched out her first plan for the book when she was living intimately with a family as awesomely conscientious as the Tyrolds themselves, namely that of George III and Queen Charlotte, and was herself living out a grim commitment to duty. Some aspects of the Tyrold family life draw more closely on the royal family than on the Burneys. Queen Charlotte was a conscientious mother like Mrs Tyrold, who ruthlessly sacrificed herself to duty, repressed her female children and was distressed by unruly sons. In her many hours with the Queen, Burney saw and felt her relentless exaction of duty on herself and everyone around. Burney could also contrast the deserving, repressed royal daughters with their licentious brothers. While the three Tyrold girls are models of good conduct and at the same time terrified of disappointing their parents, Lionel is totally self-indulgent and thoughtless of others, and for the most part gets away with it. He constantly plays witless practical jokes on his sisters, which cause them pain and embarrassment but are not reproved by them or anyone else. Though he is the oldest of the Tyrold children, he shows the least responsibility and self-control. He squanders a relatively large allowance while his sisters worry over shillings, and then he pressures them into lending him money. Even his actual crimes, extortion and adultery, occasion him only temporary punishment and minimal remorse, in contrast to Camilla's agonies over excusable errors in judgment.

Lionel is primarily, of course, an exaggerated projection of the Burney brothers, one of whom had shamed the family by stealing books from the Cambridge University library and one had been packed off to India for some unknown crime; another, James, used to make fun of Frances by publicly displaying her inability to read at the age of eight (*Memoirs* 168).[21] She expressed through Lionel her anger at the unfair privileges and indulgence given to boys, although, significantly, her book criticizes him for his offenses against his parents rather than his sisters.

Burney provides Camilla with wise and loving parents who are models of Christian virtue themselves and work tirelessly to inculcate it in their children. Although Camilla is sweet, virtuous and well-behaved, her gaiety and thoughtlessness inspire them with constant apprehension; and Burney's plot confirms their fears. Camilla means well, but when she leaves the parental home to take a trip with a friend, she makes a series of increasingly disastrous mistakes. Instead of learning from these to make judicious decisions, she learns to do nothing without her parents' guidance, and is rewarded with their love and approval. Self-possession was part of Cecilia's excellence; the least self-confidence on Camilla's part gets her into trouble.

Camilla is constantly being judged and found wanting, particularly by the man she loves. This is Edgar Mandlebert, her father's ward, a rich young man with awesome personal qualities: he has looks and manners to delight the young together with morals and conduct to delight the most old and respectable (57).[22] From his first appearance at the age of thirteen, he demonstrates a judgment and presence of mind superior to that of the elderly squire Sir Hugh Tyrold. His obvious and conscious virtue leads everyone, including himself, to accept his constant evaluation as prudent, judicious concern. He is always giving Camilla wise advice; when, through imprudence, compounded by unfortunate circumstances, she fails to follow it, she invariably comes to grief. When she makes some ill-advised attempts to stimulate his interest by flirtation with other men, he concludes that she is culpably light-minded and leaves her. But ultimately he realizes her single-minded devotion to him, repudiates his suspicions, and takes her back. She looks forward to wedded bliss, protected from further mistakes and distress by the supervision of her parents and Edgar.

Thus *Camilla* appears to be preaching a dismally repressive message, marking a regression from *Cecilia*, which shows a young woman capable of running her own life, deplores the social forces that prevent her from doing so, and deflates established authority. In *Cecilia* it was benighted old Mr Delvile who decreed that the heroine had no occasion to buy books because she could use her husband's library when she got married (186); in *Camilla* it is Camilla's wise, virtuous father who assumes that a woman has no need to develop her mind for her own sake. Mr Tyrold tells his daughter, in a long sermon-letter that is obviously a set piece, that it is impossible to know how to educate a girl, because what is right for her is determined by 'the humour of the husband into whose hands she may fall' (357). His letter rationalizes the enforced dependency of women that *Cecilia* protests, and it firmly enlists reason on the side of female repression, as Burney had criticized Mrs Delvile for doing. Good sense will show Camilla 'the power of self-conquest', and 'point out its means'. It will

> instruct you to curb those unguarded movements which lay you open to the strictures of others. It will talk to you of those boundaries which custom forbids your sex to pass, and the hazard of any individual attempt to transgress them. It will tell you, that where allowed only a negative choice [in marriage partner], it is your own best interest to combat against a positive wish. (358–9)

Women's reason is to be used to facilitate self-conquest, to alert them to the power of public opinion and custom, to warn them of the consequences of nonconformity, to resign them to accept the status quo as unchangeable. They could not reject any of these consequences without giving up their claim to be reasonable. Self-respect is made to depend on self-repression.

However, as Margaret Doody has conclusively proved, this reading cannot be accepted at face value. She points to contradictory clues, which indicate that every character in the book, including Edgar and the Tyrold parents, makes mistakes; Mr Tyrold's well-meant advice to his daughter produces disastrous consequences, for it keeps her from revealing the love that Edgar must be confident of before he will propose. Doody notes that certain opinions that might seem to be those of the omniscient narrator are actually renditions in indirect discourse of the thoughts of a character, who may be intended to be mistaken. This is particularly true of Edgar's judgments on Camilla: his complaints of her levity or untruthfulness are often his erroneous impressions rather than authorial statements (*Burney* 257). Far from preaching a conventional morality based on simplistic moral judgments, Doody argues, Burney developed her story to demonstrate the impossibility of understanding the human heart and the consequent errors produced by judging others.

The central relationships in *Camilla* are indeed problematic, complicated by misunderstandings and misjudgments produced by the characters' perversities and biases, deficiencies and excesses. Mrs Tyrold is an eminently capable, well-intentioned, virtuous woman, yet her rigid idealism damages others, as well as herself. Her profound respect for and obedience to her husband were only what was expected of eighteenth-century wives. Hester Mulso (Chapone) affirmed that 'a husband has a divine right to the absolute obedience of his wife,' although she went on to mitigate this principle by stipulating that a generous man would respect his wife enough to treat her as an equal and that she for one 'would not marry a man, upon whose generosity I could not absolutely depend' (*Works* 2:118–23). This is exactly what Mrs Tyrold has done. However, Burney's formulation of Mrs Tyrold's standard is phrased to suggest self-repression bordering on masochism:

> Had this lady been united to a man whom she despised, she would yet have obeyed him, and as scrupulously, though not as happily, as she obeyed her honoured partner . . . no dissent in opinion exculpated, in her mind, the least deviation from his will. (13–14)

Moreover, her idolization of her husband causes her to undervalue everyone else. In describing the wonderfully harmonious relationship between the couple, Burney hints at a tendency to censoriousness and rigid perfectionism in Mrs Tyrold and, even more delicately, at weakness in her husband: 'Mr. Tyrold revered while he softened the rigid virtues of his wife, who adored while she fortified the melting humanity of her husband' (9).

Mrs Tyrold is admirably clear-sighted and superior to senti-mental weakness and wishful thinking, but her reason can be too incisive. Confronted with the painful muddle of Camilla's feelings for Edgar – she worshipfully loves him, even though he has left her for reasons no one can understand – Mrs Tyrold demands clarification that cannot be forthcoming:

> If Edgar has merited well of you, why are you parted? – If ill – why this solicitude my opinion of him should be unshaken? . . . Speak out, then, and speak clearer, my dearest Camilla. If you think of him so well, and are so sure of his good intentions, what – in two words, – what is it that has parted you? (895; Epstein 136)

On the one hand, she is trying to introduce a directness and clarity that could save the young people much grief. On the other, she insists on oversimplifying a complicated situation and penetrating relentlessly into a sensitive area.

Applying her reason to Sir Hugh's fuzzy mental processes leads her to pointlessly destructive judgment. When he fat-uously conceives that learning the classics would be possible at his age and would make him happy, Mr Tyrold quietly co-operates with the plan because it is harmless, but not so Mrs Tyrold: 'In the award of cool reason, to attend to what is im-practicable, appears a folly which no inducement can excuse.' So contemptuous was she of this 'false indulgence of childish vanity' that (despite her veneration for her husband) 'her understanding felt shocked that Mr. Tyrold would deign to humour his brother in an enterprise which must inevitably terminate in a fruitless consumption of time.' Concerned only with rational theory, she ignores the fact that Sir Hugh has nothing else to do. Moreover, 'a high superiority to all deceit' keeps her from concealing her opinion from its object (35). Her virtuous principles do not stimulate her to be forbearing or kind to Sir Hugh or even to recognize his goodness: she 'almost undisguisedly' despises his hopes and his fears (152). So uncharitable is she that she thinks him too foolish to appreciate sweetness and kindness in others: she opposes the plan that Camilla live with him, on the grounds that it would be 'reposing a trust so precious where its value could so ill be appreciated' (13). Seemingly an expression of cherishing concern, this is in fact a rationalization for keeping total control over her daughter and limiting her pleasure. Mrs Tyrold's virtue expresses itself in an instinctive suspicion of the enjoyable living in Sir Hugh's easygoing household, his generous appreciation of others and the advantage of inheriting his fortune.

Yet it is clear that she is the more competent parent. Everything goes wrong when she leaves the house, called by duty to Lisbon; and the situation cannot be straightened out until she returns to the scene. Camilla knows that she could not conceal her debts from her mother as she has from her father. He (like Dr Burney) is not very observant, but she notices everything, even when overwhelmed with business (217).[23] Her ineluctable penetration and refusal to be swayed by sentiment make her frightening, but are associated with her competence. Wholly nurturant maternal figures in Burney, such as Mrs Charlton in *Cecilia* and Mrs Mirvan in *Evelina*, are ineffectual. It is Mrs Tyrold, not her husband, who enforces the rigorous discipline of the household. Burney assures us that she was 'unaffectedly beloved,' but also 'deeply feared by all her children, Camilla alone excepted' (238; the latter claim is constantly belied by the story). This fear was not necessarily deplorable by eighteenth-century standards, when ideals of family relationships were radically different from ours: what seems self-evidently harsh today was then considered salutary.

Most eighteenth-century authorities agreed that strict discipline was more important than affection. Hannah More, who believed children were inherently corrupt, reprobated those who elevated sentiment and sympathy over principle (1:67). But even Mary Wollstonecraft would have supported Mrs Tyrold's policies. She warned against yielding 'to the present impulse of tenderness or compassion' and concluded:

> Severity is frequently the most certain as well as the most sublime proof of affection; and the want of this power over the feelings, and of that lofty, dignified affection, which makes a person prefer the future good of the beloved object to a present gratification, is the reason why so many fond mothers spoil their children. (*Vindication* 161)

On the other hand, Mrs Tyrold's rigor does seem to have unfortunate effects on her children. Camilla's mistakes result from an education that has prevented her from developing self-reliance by keeping her dependent on parental approval. She is afraid to tell her parents about problems that reveal her imperfection, and yet she feels she has no excuse for failing to act correctly, because of the high standards they have taught and she has internalized. At the age of twelve Camilla's sister Lavinia, whose character is defined by blamelessness, is tortured by remorse because the fun of a party has caused her to forget an order of her mother's. Eugenia, the third sister, insists on making and keeping to her disastrous marriage because the morality of self-sacrifice and blind adherence to principle has been drilled into her. And brother Lionel's sins may well have been aggravated by rebellion against impossibly high parental standards. All the children suffer from a sense of inadequacy because their parents have imposed on them moral standards too high for any mortal child to fulfill.

Burney did not pursue the Tyrold method in her own family. Although she did not openly dispute her husband's authority, she clearly considered her own judgment better and generally got her way. When he happily wrote from France that he had arranged a marriage with a French girl for their twenty-one-year-old son, she demolished his plan with quiet logic. Her attitude toward child-rearing was different and wiser than Mrs Tyrold's, or at least became so. Drawing from years of experience that neither More nor Wollstonecraft nor she herself had at the time of writing *Camilla* (when her son was an infant), she explained to her husband why his plan of reforming their shiftless son by an ultimatum could not work:

> He is not *capable*, mon ami, of an exactitude of that Undeviating Character. To force further *solemn promises* from so forgetful, so unreflecting, yet so undesigning & well meaning a Young Creature . . . instead of frightening him into *right*, would harden him into *desperation*. (*JL* 10:669)

Mrs Tyrold emerges as a penetrating study in the destructive effects of misdirected love and virtue. Burney developed in her what she had sketched in Mrs Delvile, who 'rather idolised than loved' her son (462) and for that very reason was prepared to sacrifice his well-being to her ideal of him. Mrs Tyrold loves Camilla with intensity – having idolized her from birth 'in her inmost soul' (882). Yet she shows her love by relentlessly striving to force the child into her mold of perfection: Camilla sees only kindness in her mother's attitude, but does recognize it as 'a kindness that, even from my childhood, seemed to say, Camilla, be blameless – or you break your Mother's heart!' With such expectations, it is no wonder that her 'poor unhappy Mother . . . has always seemed to have a presentiment, I was born to bring her to sorrow!' (866). Unfortunately, it is poor unhappy Camilla who must bear the guilt. This awesome perfectionist – demanding of herself implicit obedience to her husband and eternal vigilance over her children – is equally demanding on her daughters.

Edgar, apparently so totally admirable, is revealed to be both rigid and insecure. Burney's portrayal of his relationship with Camilla shows penetrating psychological insight as she develops Edgar's domination and Camilla's anxious dependency. Edgar punctiliously lives up to his own high standards and can be delicately thoughtful and considerate when he understands a situation – as when he covers Camilla's embarrassment at winning a raffled locket after he has pressured her to withdraw her subscription (124–5) – but his sympathy and understanding are severely limited. His practice of seeing people's every imperfection but equally noticing their every merit (57) sounds just and reasonable until we see him watching Camilla, the woman who loves him and whom he supposedly loves in return. Far from Edgar is the lover's tendency 'to transfuse all that he himself most prizes, and thinks praise-worthy, into the breast of his chosen object' (801). Rather, he watches anxiously to see whether she is worthy of him. On the occasion of a public breakfast, he notices and approves her kindness to a poor prisoner's wife; but he also notices that, having initially abstained from the raffle for the locket, she then follows the example of her fascinating new friend Mrs Arlbery and puts in her money: 'Edgar, disappointed, retreated in silence' (94). When Camilla does not stay in a shop to hear an expressive reading of James Thomson's description of conjugal felicity, Edgar wonders 'how she could absent herself from hearing what so well was worth her studying' (101). When she reveals temporary agitation by entangling the sewing silk she is supposed to be winding, he wonders whether her lack of self-control is a constitutional failing (171).

Moreover, his values are perversely misplaced, and in such a way that the qualities Camilla lacks seem to him more important than those she has. He is properly enchanted with her affection and concern for her uncle during his critical illness, but what looms greater in his mind is 'the unaccountable circumstance of her starting forth from a back seat at the play, where she had sat concealed, attended by the Major, and without any matron protectress' (326–7). She had gone with Mrs Arlbery, who had left early; had been prevented by chance from immediately joining another matron; and had concealed herself from a well-grounded fear of Edgar's censure.

Nevertheless, when he confronted her with his concern, 'She thanked him for remembering his character of her monitor, and acknowledged the fault to be her own, with a candour so unaffected' and a 'soft seriousness' which 'captivated' him (339).

What really gratifies Edgar is to see Camilla apologizing or giving up something she would like to do simply because he advises against it, without giving any reason. Thus Burney hints at the need for power over his love object that lurks under Edgar's watchful solicitude. Edgar's power drive, expressed particularly in his need to test the woman he loves, makes him a sort of domesticated Lovelace – more frightening because closer to what was normal and approved in his culture. Like Lovelace, Edgar cannot simply accept and rejoice in his love object as she really is – sweet, kind, ingenuous, loving and eager to please. He must search for hidden flaws and keep testing her, while he withholds commitment and security, and thereby leaves her more vulnerable to influences that may lead her astray. If she passes one test, there is always another for her to fail. Moreover, some of the tests cannot be passed because they subject her to demands that are incompatible with his own standards or those that have been inculcated in her by exemplary parents.

Edgar's unloving tendencies are reinforced by his mentor, Dr Marchmont, an apparently exemplary man who keeps giving him what seem to be sensible cautions about making sure Camilla has the requisites to make him happy. Doody points out how artfully Burney sets him up as reasonable and then exposes the emotional basis of his arguments: namely, that he has been soured on women by his experience with two wives who failed to give him the devotion he expected (*Burney* 225). Marchmont is the most pernicious type of misogynist, since his ungenerous suspicions and unsupported charges against women are concealed by his general appearance of virtue, wisdom and good social adjustment. He is constantly contrasted with Dr Orkborne, a self-centered, ill-bred pedant who openly despises women. Everybody laughs at Orkborne, while everybody listens respectfully to Marchmont. Hence he is in a good position to reinforce the self-centeredness that Edgar would pick up from his patriarchal culture and the cautious hesitancy that marks his personal character.

Immediately after representing Camilla expressing her uncritical love for Edgar and pitying him for his apparent future of marriage to Indiana (which would be, of course, entirely his own fault), Burney shows us Edgar and Dr Marchmont considering her character and fate with cold-blooded, self-centered prudence. At first Edgar expresses his delighted appreciation of her sweetness and charm, demonstrated by her giving up a much-desired visit to Mrs Arlbery simply because he disapproved. But then Marchmont urges him not to declare his passion or let it appear until he knows her heart more thoroughly; for Edgar is too valuable to be 'thrown away' upon a woman who is not fully worthy of him. Even though Edgar has known her from a child, Marchmont insists that yet more evidence is needed. A potential wife must be more carefully scrutinized than women in general: 'Whatever she does,' or says, he tells Edgar,

> you must ask yourself this question: 'Should I like such behaviour in my wife:' . . . even justice is insufficient during this period of probation, and instead of inquiring, 'Is this right in her?' you must simply ask, 'Would it be pleasing to me?' (158–60)

The appalling self-centeredness passes without notice because it conforms to the assumption of the time that a desirable young man is entitled to put a woman through a probationary period to make sure that she will satisfy him. No one, least of all she herself, considers whether he will satisfy Camilla. Eighteenth-century society placed man at the center, expected woman to meet his needs, and assumed his right to judge whether she did.

If Marchmont cannot find something to censure in women's actual behavior, he finds something to suspect in their motives. When Edgar fears that Camilla will prefer Hal Westwyn to him because Hal was ready to duel for her, Marchmont confirms his fear; when Edgar says this would at least prove that she is not mercenary, since Hal is not rich, Marchmont will not admit it:

> This does not, necessarily, prove her disinterested; she is too young, yet, to know herself the value she may hereafter set upon wealth. And . . . there is commonly so little stability . . . in the female character, that any sudden glare of adventitious lure, will draw them, for the moment, from any and every regular plan of substantial benefit. (654)

If Camilla considers Edgar's fortune in accepting him, she should be rejected for impure motives; if she does not care about fortune, she should be despised for levity. Edgar recognizes that Marchmont is prejudiced, but evidently finds his reasoning too congenial to reject.

Marchmont further insists that Camilla must demonstrate devotion as well as virtue before Edgar commits himself by declaring his love: she must make clear that she prefers him to all other men and loves him for himself alone. A man should not propose marriage without being absolutely sure of 'the entire possession' of the woman's heart and 'the complete knowledge of her disposition' (645). Even if Edgar is absolutely right about Camilla's character and disposition, he may not have the love he 'deserves' from her: suppose she should accept him because of family pressure, the normal female desire for marriage, and his wealth? Marchmont glibly supposes it possible to sort out the motives for a woman's partiality with the accuracy of a chemical analysis – as if it could be perfectly clear how much was spontaneous love, how much response to the man's declaration, how much liking for his fortune and situation (178–9). How much wiser was Jane

Austen in making Elizabeth Bennet appreciate both Darcy and Pemberley, and in accepting this as human nature.

Marchmont's superficially rational attitude was particularly unfair in the light of women's circumstances at the time. He makes them appear mercenary and trivial when he rightly charges that 'half the married women in the nation . . . became wives' because

> their friends urged them; . . . they had no other establishment in view; . . . nothing is so uncertain as the repetition of matrimonial powers in women; . . . and . . . those who cannot solicit what they wish, must accommodate themselves to what offers. (643–4)

What he ignores, of course, is that few women were in a position to be superior to all considerations but love. Moreover, moralists like the actual Dr Gregory and the fictional Mr Tyrold told women that it was their duty to accept gracefully such men and circumstances as presented themselves. Burney saw marriages of convenience all around her, and, in the Barlow affair, had feared she might succumb to exactly the pressures Marchmont lists.

So Edgar withholds his proposal, feeling perfectly justified because he has never explicitly declared himself, just as Cambridge and Digby had led Burney to expect a proposal and then left her, apparently without feeling guilt. Meanwhile, he is constantly drawing conclusions from her manner. Neither he nor Marchmont could bear the thought of being (conventionally) dishonorable; but neither sees that feelings can create obligations, that a man has a responsibility to a woman whom he has led to fall in love with him. Recognizing moral obligation only in the form of moral law, Edgar believes he may blamelessly abandon Camilla should she fail to measure up to his expectations, regardless of her feelings.

Moreover, he is too self-centered to realize that, as the less experienced and independent of the two, she is less able to assess his feelings and more needs to know them. (This is a literal rendition of Cecilia's situation at the masquerade, surrounded by disguised men.) Even more unfairly, Edgar expects her to guess his undeclared love; for he blames her for civility to other men, which he has himself provoked by his apparent indifference. He demands devoted constancy from her while giving her no evidence that his feelings make it appropriate. If Camilla were to show her love, of course, she would almost certainly offend Edgar's fastidious standards of feminine delicacy. Her mother, we are explicitly told, 'gloried in the virtuous delicacy of her daughter, that so properly, till it was called for, concealed her tenderness from the object who so deservingly inspired it' (237). Camilla cannot win.

Marchmont's warnings operate because Edgar, despite his excellency, is insecure. Burney presents this sympathetically:

> Mandlebert, filled now with a distrust of himself and his powers, which he was incapable of harbouring of Camilla . . . felt struck to the soul with the apprehension of failing to gain her affection, and wounded in every point both of honour and delicacy, from the bare suggestion of owing his wife to his situation in the world . . . his confidence was gone; his elevation of sentiment was depressed. (161–2)

He is perhaps to be pitied, since he is unhappy and too diffident to realize that he is responsible for the situation. But what is more striking is the ruinous consequences that male insecurity lays on women: not only does Edgar withhold his declaration of love, but he is perpetually ready to believe that Camilla prefers some other man, no matter how much evidence there is that she adores Edgar. Burney clearly demonstrates that jealousy comes more from the insecurity of the jealous person than from the suspected person's behavior. Yet, in a society where men's perceptions prevail, women will be victimized by men's suspicions with or without justification.

It is natural that a girl brought up like Camilla would fall in love with a masterful man like Edgar and become pathetically dependent on him. His position of superiority is confirmed in every way. He is rich and independent, while she has no way of making her own happiness. Edgar's money not only gives him a superior position in the marriage market, it gives him moral superiority as well. Camilla is as charitable as he is, but his gifts can be larger and therefore more impressive: while she must deprive herself to give a few shillings, he can set a poor family up in a cottage without feeling it, and she adores his generosity.

She delights in considering him 'a younger Mr. Tyrold' (742) and reverences his moral authority in the same way. Thus he exerts a deeper control over her than Delvile or even Orville exert over their ladies; her attitude is that of a dutiful daughter rather than of a young woman who is choosing whether she will commit herself to marriage. She confesses to Edgar her consuming guilt for having spent half a guinea on the raffle and thus leaving herself only a shilling to give some poor people, imagining what her father would have said if he knew; Edgar is 'charmed with her penitence, though joining in the apprehended censure' (98). Edgar's character and his attitude toward Camilla reinforce the parental constraints; he has the same hold over her superego as her parents do. Even when they have parted forever, as she believes, she tries 'to make all his opinions and counsels the rule and measure of her conduct' (793). Edgar controls Camilla subtly, telling her he does not mean to enforce his advice, 'but merely to offer hints – intimations – and observations – that without controlling, may put you upon your guard' (475). But, after the training she has received, hints from Edgar, as from her parents, have the force of commands; so the distinction is meaningless. The authorities can enforce their will without incurring the odium of coercing a human being who should be free.

Camilla encourages Edgar's judgmental attitude because

she is young and inexperienced, and because she has been trained to turn to her elders for guidance and to doubt her own impulses and perceptions. It never occurs to her to question his judgment or to criticize him; she perpetually asks for his guidance, tries to follow it, and earns his approval for doing so.[24] Her weak self-esteem causes her to overestimate his superiority and renders her unable to resist him. Although Burney never explicitly criticizes this state of affairs, she does recognize the advantage it gives to Edgar: 'Nothing gives so much strength to an adversary as the view of timidity in his opponent. Edgar grew presently composed, and felt equal to his purposed expostulation' (617).

Camilla's inability to assert herself causes her to be misjudged and dominated. So does her liability to guilt. Although Camilla's upbringing makes her particularly liable, Burney saw guilt as characteristic of women in general, resulting from a morality that focused on errors committed rather than goodness shown and, paradoxically, from women's powerlessness. Often women could not control their actions, but were kept from right or forced into wrong by external forces. And yet they were held, and held themselves, just as accountable as if they were in control of their lives. Though deprived of legal and economic power, though deprived of the power that comes from knowledge of the world, though encouraged to conform and to respect authority without question, women, including young ones, were held as morally responsible as men. Burney's heroines feel guilt for associating with people they cannot avoid, for spending money when there is no way to save it, for taking demeaning or improper work when they need it to support themselves, for being the passive occasion for sexual suspicions.

Despite her lifelong conscientiousness and devotion to duty, Burney herself suffered from guilt, resulting from her perfectionism and from the conflict between her need to express herself in writing and her need to avoid blame by passivity. She

86

expressed this dilemma in her fictional heroines, who are equally conscientious, by placing them in situations where they must act and then showing the unfortunate consequences of that action. Because she must operate within externally imposed constrictions, Cecilia's good judgment and good intentions cannot protect her from choices that will produce wrong and guilt. As she is enmeshed in giving the Harrels money, she is torn between pity for them, intensified by the man's suicide threats, and the knowledge that she is squandering her money irresponsibly: 'perplexity and uneasiness, regret and resentment, accompanied the donation' (393).

She suffers remorse when Belfield and Floyer duel over her, despite having done nothing to provoke the duel and everything she could to prevent it. As the two men competed for the honor of escorting her from the Opera-House, each more interested in maintaining his manly honor than in helping her, she was the passive object of their contention. Her attempt to prevent a quarrel had no effect except to convince the bystanders that she was in love with one of the men. Yet, when she heard of Belfield's prolonged sufferings from his wound, she 'accused herself with much bitterness' for having brought the duel on (212).[25]

Cecilia was practically forced into her secret marriage by Delvile's importunity on the one hand and his parents' intransigence about the required name change on the other, but, as soon as she reluctantly agreed, she was overwhelmed by guilt: 'the step she was now about to take, all her principles opposed; it terrified her as undutiful, it shocked her as clandestine . . . she regretted her consent to it as the loss of her self-esteem, and believed, even if a reconciliation took place,' she would have a permanent blemish on her character that would 'be a constant allay to her happiness, by telling her how unworthily she had obtained it' (576). Her guilt causes her to vacillate between consent and withdrawal and drives her to comply with Mrs Delvile's extortionate demand to meet Mortimer so as to give him up in person; then, since she had agreed to part, she condemns herself for giving way to sorrow in his presence: 'a weak effusion of tenderness, injurious to delicacy, and censurable by propriety.' This lapse, natural and virtually irresistible, moves her to an even more sweeping self-condemnation:

> All she had done she now repented, all she had said she disapproved; her conduct, seldom equal to her notions of right, was now infinitely below them, and the reproaches of her judgment made her forget for awhile the afflictions which had misled it. (645)

Even misfortune makes her feel guilty, since it attracts unfavorable notice. When Cecilia is ejected from her home for becoming Mrs Mortimer Delvile, she finds herself, for the first time in her life, short of money and totally alone. She is not only anxious and unhappy, but ashamed:

> by this unforeseen vicissitude of fortune, she was suddenly, from being an object of envy and admiration, sunk into distress, and threatened with disgrace; from being every where caressed, and by every voice praised, she blushed to be seen, and expected to be censured; and, from being generally regarded as an example of happiness, and a model of virtue, she was now in one moment to appear to the world, an outcast from her own house, yet received into no other! a bride, unclaimed by a husband! an HEIRESS, dispossessed of all wealth! (868–9)

Loss of money causes loss of social position, and the consequent loss of respect extends from social to moral shame; taught to believe that a really virtuous woman was one whom nobody criticized and that it was possible to avoid criticism if she behaved properly, Cecilia cannot help feeling that she has somehow done something wrong.

Camilla is more constantly guilty than Cecilia, partly because she does make more errors, but mostly because she lacks confidence and self-esteem. Her involvement in a threatened duel is as innocent as Cecilia's and more heavily burdened by remorse. When she is walking around Southampton with Mrs Mittin, simply because she lacks the self-assurance to get rid of her, Mittin's forward curiosity causes the shopkeepers to stare after them and they become an object of public notice and speculation. This leads to a dispute over Camilla's good character, and a chivalrous young man, Hal Westwyn, ends up defending her virtue by a challenge. Camilla's behavior was obviously not immoral and not even particularly imprudent – although Edgar does deplore her going about accompanied only by an ill-bred person – but it leads to serious consequences and remorse.

> Should the duel take place, and any fatal consequences follow, she felt she should never be happy again; and even, should it be prevented, its very suggestion, from so horrible a doubt of her character, seemed a stain from which it could never recover. The inconsiderate facility with which she had wandered about with a person so little known to her, so underbred, and so forward, appeared now to herself inexcusable; and she determined, if but spared this dreadful punishment, to pass the whole of her future life in unremitting caution.

When the young man's kindly father speaks to her, she almost faints in her chair because she feels herself to be the murderer of his son (637). Camilla is trapped into actions of which she could not possibly see the consequences, and yet she holds herself responsible for them. She is blamed, although it is the young man who actually has acted imprudently and inconsiderately. This episode brings out very well the way in which minor errors in judgment can combine with bad luck and other people's misbehavior to produce an appearance of guilt and consequent remorse in a susceptible person.

Most often, Camilla's guilt arises in the more common area of spending money, an area in which women were notably deprived of power and yet forced to act. They had to spend money, but were severely limited both in what they had and in their opportunities to acquire more. All they could do was save, and Burney shows through Camilla that even that was sometimes impossible. Although women have been tradition-ally censured for wasting men's money, Burney shows how they may be forced to spend on what appear to be self-indulgent luxuries. When Camilla gives money for fashionable clothes or amusements at Tunbridge, it is because she feels she must. In part she is right; Burney herself had learned how expensive it was for a lady to make a decent appearance in society. But also, simply because Camilla is inexperienced, she mistakenly believes some outlays are obligatory, does not know how much things cost, is embarrassed to discuss her financial problems. Her first financial imprudence was letting Lionel pressure her into giving him the twenty pounds spend-ing money she received for her trip. Yet here, as usual, she was conforming to traditional standards for feminine behavior; for sisters were supposed to put their brothers' interests first.

And yet Camilla is made to feel as guilty as the most irre-sponsible spendthrift, even though almost none of the money has gone to give her pleasure. At Southampton she forgoes new clothes even when her wardrobe becomes embarrassingly un-fashionable and shabby. Yet no amount of saving can clear her debts. She is almost forced into her disastrous transaction with the professional moneylender by her reluctance to add to the financial worries of her father and uncle, caused by the far greater debts of her brother and male cousin, and by her wish not to keep tradesmen waiting for their just payment. Camilla is inexorably stripped of her money as Cecilia is, but on a piti-fully smaller, and more realistic, scale.

Even Camilla's goodness contributes to her guilt: she strives to maintain everyone's approval, but in pleasing one person she may have to disoblige another. By wrongly accusing her of attracting Edgar's affections away from Indiana to herself, Miss Margland forces her into a position where she can only clear herself by flouting his wish that she stay away from Mrs Arlbery. So she miserably resolves on the visit, Edgar finds out and is mortified by her apparent indifference to his wishes, and she feels 'agony' for having 'ungratefully' offended him: 'I can only convince them of my innocence by acting towards Edgar as a monster. – Ah! I would sooner a thousand times let them all think me guilty!' (182). Burney sets up situation after situation in which, through no fault of her own, Camilla seems to be disregarding his wishes. When her hostess's party decides to go to a show of performing monkeys, Edgar indicates that a young lady should not want to attend such a thing; and Camilla immediately volunteers to give up the idea. Then she is brought there unawares and forced inside to oblige the rest of the company. Edgar comes to see whether she has obeyed him, finds her there, and is displeased; and so she has to apologize, as usual. Thus he is chronically censorious, and she feels chronically guilty.

Camilla's guilt is aggravated by her inability to live up to the standards and models of perfection set up by her parents. Thoughts of their excellence and strenuous moral training intensify her remorse after any mistake. She heaps condemnation upon herself for failing her mother, who has striven 'to guard her poor tottering girl from evil,' and her father, who has been superlatively good to her (786). Camilla's parents require of her the same inhuman restraint on emotion that Cecilia required of herself. When her father discovers her seemingly unrequited love for Edgar, he exhorts her to avoid the least sign of particular affection. She must not even show reserve, which would betray resentment at disappointed love. If she cannot maintain this course toward a man she loves, he declares, she will be inexcusably lacking in good sense and self-respect.

He blandly moves on from the difficult to the self-contradictory. Although she must pursue a course that requires constant calculation and concealment of her feelings, she must not be hypocritical. Discretion, he asserts, is 'a conciliation to virtue,' and is to be distinguished from hypocrisy (361). This glaring inconsistency was as invisible to actual eighteenth-century moralists as it was to Mr Tyrold. Gregory exhorted his daughters to conceal sedulously not only their wit and learning, but even their good sense, good health, and love for their husbands – and then told them he wished them 'to possess the most perfect simplicity of heart and manners' (45).[26]

Camilla not only accepts her father's draconian advice at face value, but so adores him that she responds to it by calling him the 'most lenient of human beings' (as Burney was grateful for her father's kindness after he had tormented her for hours about her carelessness with her diary). Camilla is so moved by her father's leniency that she resolves to 'hide till I can conquer this weak emotion, and no one shall ever know . . . that a daughter of yours has a feeling she ought to disguise!' (345) When she is surprised by an accident into revealing her intense concern for Edgar, she is overcome with shame at not being able to suppress feelings her father 'had enjoined her to combat . . . how could she hope for his pardon? or how obtain her own, to have forfeited an approbation so precious?' (347)

The fact that *ought* can apply either in the prudential or the moral realm points to an ambiguity in the female code of conduct that increases Camilla's guilt and confusion, as she experiences regret for imprudence as if it were remorse for sin. It could be justifiably argued on prudential grounds that Camilla ought to disguise her feelings (since the Tyrolds do not share the reader's knowledge of what is going on in Edgar's mind), but this is not a moral issue. Because she thinks it is, her father's advice takes on a sacred character; and her own inability to follow it generates deep feelings of unworthiness. Although he constantly acknowledges the superiority of virtue to prudence, his strictures suggest that prudence is the all-important moral law.

From the prudential point of view, reputation is more important than virtue. Letting 'an unreturned female regard' be seen 'is commonly, however ungenerously, imagined rather to indicate ungoverned passions, than refined selection.' Mr Tyrold suggests that 'the woman who has permitted it to go abroad' cannot 'reasonably demand that consideration and respect from the community, in which she has been wanting to herself' (361). Unkind misinterpretation slides imperceptibly into just condemnation of failing, and public opinion takes on the force of moral law. It may be an ungenerous error to attribute unrequited love in a woman to ungoverned passions, but if she reveals it, she is rightly disgraced. In effect, then, unreturned love is as guilty as raging lust. This confusion concerning moral guilt, imprudence, deviation from convention and the attracting of unfavorable public comment kept women perpetually guilty and increased the hold that respected authorities held over them. A hint of impropriety or general disapprobation could have the force of the heaviest moral warning.

It is significant that the Burney heroine who suffers the most guilt is the one with the least power. The others may be frustrated, but they do form plans and pursue them. Camilla lacks the ego-strength to do more than try to meet other people's demands. Again and again, she is driven into action by external forces – when she goes to places Edgar disapproves of, when she pays a guinea subscription she cannot afford, when she continues seeing Sir Sedley Clarendel. Although she is constantly sacrificing her own interests to those of others, she feels a guilt appropriate to the most self-indulgent egotist. Burney thus shows that guilt derives not so much from wrongdoing as from extreme conscientiousness and a feeling of inadequacy, both encouraged by over-demanding authority figures.

These authorities ultimately destroy the little independence Camilla gained by entering the world. After her anxiety, guilt, isolation and illness, she is received back 'to the paternal arms – to her home – to peace – to safety – and primaeval joy' (893). She regains 'her pristine confidence, and fearless ease' (894). She assures her mother, 'I shall want no fortitude . . . now again under your protection! I will scarcely even think, my beloved Mother, but by your guidance!' (895) The last paragraph of *Camilla: or A Picture of Youth* indicates that 'her virtues, her errours, her facility, or her desperation' were merely the result of her youth (913). This formulation suggests a plot in which experience would have taught her to overcome her deficiencies and deal more effectively with life's problems. But in fact, she has learned only that she cannot function on her own: instead of becoming an adult, she becomes a permanent ward of her parents and Edgar.

Divested of its saccharine rhetoric, the conclusion of *Camilla* is psychologically realistic. A child repressed and molded as Camilla has been will either rebel – as Burney was afraid her son would do – or be stripped of all spirit and possibility of becoming a mature, autonomous human being. Unfortunately, however, Burney presents the ending as happy. In *Camilla*, she realistically shows us an amiable young woman subjected by an obviously exacting mother and a subtly exacting father and consequently helpless to resist a morbidly cautious, equally exacting lover – but she indicates that the heroine will be fulfilled rather than destroyed. No limitations on the heroine's happiness are suggested, as in *Cecilia*; nor can the ending be detached as an ironic commentary on the tale, as in *The Wanderer*, where the ending makes no pretense of solving the problems raised by the story. Burney realistically portrays a relationship between a jealous, demanding man and a helplessly dependent woman; she even lets one of her characters predict precisely how deadening it will be (see below); and yet she says that it will lead to a marriage fulfilling and happy for both. Doody's reading, persuasive in so many ways, does not deal with the ending of *Camilla*.

Camilla

It seems to me that there are irreconcilable contradictions in *Camilla*, resulting from the conflict in Burney between accepting conventional morality and protesting against it. Just as she imposed a happy ending upon an irremediable situation, she glossed over the serious faults that she had exposed in conventionally virtuous characters. She emphasizes Marchmont's general wisdom and good intentions rather than his narrow sympathies and the harmful effects of his counsel. She presents the failings of Edgar and Mrs Tyrold as minor blemishes on exemplary characters. Their ideals seem intended to be right, even if we are not always intended to think them properly applied. Edgar is faulted for being a little too cautious and prone to suspicion, but not for his dreadful lack of generosity and warmth. He is criticized for leading Camilla on and keeping her in suspense, but not for his outrageous assumption that he is entitled to 'the entire possession' of her heart and 'the complete knowledge of her disposition.' Burney never comments on the disproportion between his expectations of Camilla and hers of him.

Since he is constantly judging Camilla and is only criticized for this at the end of the book, his judgmental attitude seems to be justified, even if he misreads the evidence in particular situations. It is true that Edgar ultimately makes some manly apologies for his unjust suspicions of Camilla. Once he is at last convinced that she loves him (it takes a note written on her supposed deathbed), he confesses to his habit of 'doubtfully . . . watch[ing] her every action, and suspiciously . . . judg[ing] her every motive.' But Camilla cannot wait to set his mind at rest: 'Have I any thing to forgive? I thought all apology – all explanation, rested on my part? and that my imprudencies – my rashness – my so often-erring judgment . . . and so apparently, almost even culpable conduct.' This leads to a mutual forgiveness and, in the final paragraph, to a balance between her (small) imprudence and his (great) suspicion, as if they were morally equivalent. What completes his conversion is her detailed account of her life since leaving home: 'through the whole ingenuous narration, he found himself the object of every view, the ultimate motive to every action' (900–3). In short, the ultimate result of his apology is a further reinforcement of his self-esteem. Moreover, although his doubts were all 'miraculously' removed by her letter (898), such miracles will not keep happening. Despite Burney's implication that Camilla and Edgar are embarking on a blissful marriage, there is every reason to suppose that he will continue tormenting her with his suspicions and censures.

Mrs Tyrold is a stricter version of Mrs Delvile and, like her, subjects herself to the service of patriarchy. But, though she is less flexible and less attractive, she is treated more leniently. She is never explicitly charged with faults or errors in judgment, she is not punished with an apoplectic fit, she does not recant. She is strikingly contrasted with the bad mother figure, Indiana's governess Miss Margland, who indulges her charge in order to promote her own selfish ends and whose errors in judgment are relentlessly repeated and emphasized. Miss Margland is the perpetual butt of crude jokes about her age and ugliness; she is ostentatiously officious as a chaperone, yet her incompetence is made to cause the elopements of both Indiana and Eugenia. Burney places so much distance between her good though humanly imperfect characters and her contemptible ones – she cannot say often enough that Indiana is brainless and heartless, or Miss Margland short-sighted and absurdly self-important – that the slightly flawed characters seem perfect by contrast.

If Burney had intended *Camilla* to be an attack on conventional morality, she would have exposed failings in the third major voice of authority, Mr Tyrold, and discredited the sermon-letter in which he recommends self-repression and hypocrisy to his daughter. I cannot find definite evidence that she did either. The omniscient narrator introduces Mr Tyrold as uniting all the Christian virtues – gentleness with wisdom, compassion toward others' imperfections with severity toward his own, mildness with justice (8). Nothing in the book contradicts this summary. Over and over, Burney demonstrates his charity and his practical wisdom, as well as his high principles. Although he recognizes the folly of Sir Hugh's schemes as clearly as his intolerant wife does, he encourages them because they will give Hugh innocent pleasure. More broad-minded than Edgar, he encourages Camilla's friendship with Mrs Arlbery because he hopes it will raise her spirits while Edgar is keeping her in suspense; judging as a Christian, he finds it sufficient that Arlbery is reputable, kind and charitable (257). Alone in the book, he seems to combine the virtues of reason and principle with trust, kindness and tolerance. If he errs at all, Burney implies, it would be on the side of leniency rather than repressiveness, as when he leaves his worthless son to the reproaches of his own conscience (258): he should know perfectly well that Lionel's conscience never bothers him for more than a few hours. Mrs Tyrold would have indulged in no such wishful thinking.

Mr Tyrold's letter represents his carefully considered advice. It opens with a wise and kindly argument against underestimating the seriousness of young people's sorrows and disappointments, since what counts is the suffering rather than its abstract cause (355–6). It is not possible to find a point where kindly wisdom is intended to change into stifling conventional morality. Where Burney did mean a character to be voicing both sense and nonsense, as with Hobson in *Cecilia*, she explicitly said so. It is quite possible that Mr Tyrold is supposed to be expressing an enlightened moderate position when he concedes that women undoubtedly have as much right as men to choose the marital partner they love, although he still believes they should defer to social convention, which decrees that man should choose woman and woman 'should retire to be chosen' (358). Burney would probably have agreed with him that women would be better off conforming to accepted practice than holding out for abstract rights.

External as well as internal evidence suggests that Mr Tyrold is meant to be regarded with reverence. I cannot believe that Burney could have criticized a good father. The omniscient author of *Camilla* never dissociates herself from her heroine's adoration of Mr Tyrold. Burney's dedication of her last novel to her father explicitly recalls her (anonymous) inscription of her first one to the Author of her being, and is cast in the same adulatory terms: 'With what grateful delight do I cast, now, at the same revered feet where I prostrated that first essay, this, my latest attempt!' (xvii) As far as we can tell from her letters and journals, Burney never expressed a criticism of her father, never suggested that he did not selflessly love her, never felt happy without his approval. She called him kind even when he was escorting her to her immolation in the Queen's house, resolutely oblivious to her reluctance (*DL* 2:380–1). If there was any resentment, it was too thoroughly buried to be the basis of purposeful criticism. Camilla's final promise not to think without her mother's approval almost echoes Burney's, in her letter to her father agreeing to suppress *The Witlings*, 'to have no opinion of my own in regard to what I should thenceforth part with out of my own hands' (*DL* 1:257). This submission is suspiciously extreme, but it does not express conscious resentment.

Burney indicated at the beginning and the end of *Camilla* that she meant to illustrate the impossibility of understanding people and the consequent injustice of judging them. Doody, basing her interpretation on these statements, argues that Burney's theme is that all human beings are fallible and no absolute standards (including, of course, those of conventional morality) are to be trusted. But there is much in the book that belies this coherent interpretation. Burney did make distinctions in favor of the conventionally virtuous characters. Mr Tyrold and Mrs Arlbery give Camilla well-meant advice for dealing with Edgar, he recommending the 'proper' course of modest concealment, she the 'improper' one of flirting with other men to make Edgar jealous. Both counsels turn out to be mistaken, blocking rather than promoting the romantic fulfillment; but only Mrs Arlbery's is explicitly criticized.

Burney severely punished Camilla for violating the prudence that was a major part of conventional feminine morality, and she left Edgar almost unpunished because his judgmental attitude conformed to conventional patriarchal expectations. She never probed the connection between male appropriation of judgment, male political-economic power and oppression of women. She vividly rendered passivity, vulnerability and exploitation, but did not push on to an analysis of the unjust system that caused them. She examined the effects of patriarchal ideology and repressive morality in the family, but did not criticize it there or in the society of which the family is a microcosm.

It is true that two passages in *Camilla* strongly support the interpretation that Burney meant to condemn the human tendency to make uncharitable judgments based on appearance. When Camilla is misjudged by the shopkeepers of Southampton because of the behavior of her ill-bred companion, Burney deplores 'the prevalent disposition to believe in general depravity,' not only in debased people who 'find a consolation in thinking others equally worthless,' but in good people who 'nourish a secret vanity in supposing few as good as themselves; and sully, without reflection, the fair candour of their minds, by aiding that insidious degeneracy, which robs the community of all confidence in virtue' (611). She might have been thinking of an old family friend, Mrs Ord. She liked and admired Mrs Ord, whom she even called 'maternal'; but she once remarked that 'She thinks the worst, & judges the most severely of all mankind, of any person I have ever known' (*JL* 1:49). This opinion was confirmed when Ord dropped her acquaintance because she made an unconventional marriage for love.

Burney's astute analysis of the motives and consequences of self-righteous censoriousness reflects on the most conspicuously virtuous characters in the book, and it opposes the ostensible lesson of the Southampton episode, which seems intended to illustrate Camilla's culpable lack of forethought. It is recalled in the concluding words of the whole massive work: 'What, at last, so diversified as man? what so little to be judged by his fellow?' (913) Even so, the book as a whole does not support these passages: they startle because they do not fit their context. Camilla's repeated misadventures suggest that women get misjudged because they behave incorrectly or imprudently.

Perhaps the most striking discrepancy between what Burney shows and what she says appears in her presentation of Camilla herself. Burney's conception of a lovable impulsive heroine shows her discontent with the feminine ideal of insipid propriety; the timidity of her presentation, her deference to it. Burney's stated aim was to show Camilla suffering the effects of her thoughtless imprudence and learning through 'the bitterness of personal proof alone, in suffering and in feeling, in erring and in repenting' (8). But she felt it necessary to keep her heroine's actions well within the bounds of good behavior; a proper eighteenth-century heroine could not survive serious errors. If she lost her chastity or her reputation, for example, or defied her parents, she could not be a heroine; for heroines were supposed to promote morality by being exemplars. And morality for women was restrictive and largely negative, emphasizing prudence and self-control. Mrs Tyrold exhorted Camilla to 'be blameless,' and Burney herself aspired to that condition (*JL* 10:878).

Both Evelina and Camilla are characterized as imprudent, but neither can be permitted to do anything that is culpably so. The problem is not noticeable in *Evelina*, because the heroine's 'heedless indiscretion' (341) is not emphasized, and sufficient difficulties can be produced by youth or circumstance. But in the more weighty *Camilla*, where plot developments are grounded in character, the discrepancies become glaring between what Burney says about her character and the way she makes her act, as well as between her small lapses in prudence and the severity of her punishment. Edgar's rhapsody over Camilla's original character – 'modest as she was gay, docile as she was spirited, gentle as she was intelligent' (705) – formulates Burney's aim and exposes its internal inconsistency. Aiming to unite proper femininity with endearing unconventionality, she succeeded in making only the former convincing. Exuberant gaiety, uninhibited freedom and uncalculating naturalness are not consistent with the essential propriety.

Camilla's vivacity is frequently stated, never demonstrated. Burney constantly remarks on Camilla's inability to control her impulses, but actually shows us a character who is painfully repressed, even in the strict terms of eighteenth-century decorum. Camilla begs for direction from her elders, uncritically reverences those set in authority over her, makes no claims for herself and never has a hostile feeling. She may have the name of an Amazon warrior, but she behaves herself like a proper daughter of the Tyrolds. Her culpable imprudence consists in spending small sums of money injudiciously and mildly flirting in a misguided attempt to stimulate Edgar's interest. Burney's development of her story implies that Mrs Tyrold is right to fear for Camilla's impulsiveness (120) and to believe that only marriage to the steady Edgar can preserve her from danger, but it is inconceivable that the character as drawn could do anything evil or even seriously improper.

Camilla's happy spirits, the corollary to and cause of her impulsiveness, are no more convincingly demonstrated. Burney insists on her 'youthful glee' and extreme liveliness – 'Every look was a smile, every step was a spring, every thought was a hope, every feeling was joy!' (13) – but she does not demonstrate it anywhere. She tells us that Camilla's charm 'governed her whole family' and that 'her persuasion was irresistible' (51–2), but shows her controlled by the demands of other people and her need to please them. Burney seems to be paying lip-service to the comfortable view that women could feel happy and free in eighteenth-century society, while conveying her own experience of constriction. According to popular moralists of the time, women did not experience enforced compliance as restrictive, because compliance was natural to them. Thomas Gisborne wrote that Providence, designing from the beginning that women were to be dependent on men, thoughtfully provided them with 'a remarkable tendency to conform to the wishes and example' of those they loved or even just associated with (116). If women did not mind perpetually deferring to others' wishes, restraint would not impair their joy and liveliness.

Burney's commentary also reflects the sentimental convention that uninhibited joy was the condition of female childhood, the state in which Camilla is first seen and to which she symbolically returns. Feminists like Mary Hays and conservatives like George Savile, Marquess of Halifax, agreed in idealizing girlhood lived under the protection of an indulgent father (Straub 33). To some extent, of course, women were comparatively free in this period of life, before sexual roles were rigidly defined. Burney illustrates this freedom in her description of Camilla's tenth birthday party by making her playfully change roles with Sir Hugh, the nominal head of the family (Spacks, 'Ev'ry Woman Is at Heart a Rake' 45–6).

The action of the book promptly belies this sentimental idyll, however. Lionel soon dominates the festivities, causing Eugenia to be exposed to smallpox; and Camilla's party is blighted before the day ends. From then on, she is introduced into a series of pleasure parties – and in every one she is subjected to frustration and disappointment. At her first ball, she hopes to dance with Edgar; he actually asks her four times, but each time he is prevented, by blunders which pair him with Indiana and by her own kindness in asking him to dance with the deformed Eugenia. Finally, when she might have a chance, she is monopolized by Mr Dubster, a vulgar figure of fun whom Lionel has frivolously sent over to tease her. She is too sweet and modest to be aware that she has anything to complain about, but it is evident to the reader. She is sacrificed to the convenience of others, often because she cheerfully offers to be – and does not even get credit for her self-sacrifice.

By subjecting a deserving young woman first to this string of disappointments and then to repeated experiences of disproportionate blame and remorse, Burney seems to be expressing resentment at the unfairness of woman's lot. By placing Camilla in situations where she cannot avoid guilt and exaggerating the remorse she feels for minor lapses, Burney would seem to be protesting against the ideology that set up outrageously exacting, sometimes conflicting, standards for women and then condemned women for failing to meet them (Spacks, 'Ev'ry Woman' 30). Conscientious young women were expected to repress their emotions on demand and to behave better than other people, while getting less credit. The discrepancies in the book may be intentional pointers to flaws in the theoretical system it seems to uphold.

In some cases, Camilla's estimate of herself obviously clashes with the facts of the novel, as when she equates her behavior with her brother's or sets herself far below her sister Eugenia. Although Eugenia's disastrous marriage was the result of glaring imprudence and foolish disregard of advice, it prompts Camilla to contrast her own responsibility for her misfortunes with her sister's innocence:

> Whatever she had personally to bear, she constantly imagined some imprudence or impropriety had provoked; but Eugenia, while she appeared to her so blameless, that she could merit no evil, was so amiable, that willingly she would have borne for her their united portions. (804–5)

In fact, Burney may be hinting that Camilla underrates herself through using the words *'imagined'* and *'appeared'*, as she often does when relating Camilla's self-judgments. And it may be that Camilla's excruciating remorse near the end is meant to express her over-sensibility rather than objective guilt:

> She reviewed her own conduct without mercy; and though misery after misery had followed every failing, all her sufferings appeared light to her repentant sense of her criminality; for as criminal alone, she could consider what had inflicted misfortunes upon persons so exemplary. (855–6)

Whether her remorse is meant to be an appropriate response to her errors or an outburst of adolescent self-dramatization, it provides an occasion for indulgence in melodramatic pathos, with inappropriate echoes of *Clarissa*, for a nightmare of damnation suggesting the agonizing delusions of religious melancholia (875–6), and for extraneous horrors, such as bringing a corpse into the neighboring room, who turns out to be Camilla's brother-in-law.[27]

However, many comments by the omniscient narrator do not confirm the interpretation that Burney meant to satirize conventional morality. Although she occasionally expresses sympathy, pointing out how hard it is for a girl to forgo attractive clothes just when she is entering the world, she more often condemns Camilla with rhadamanthine strictness. When Camilla flees homeward because she cannot face a deeply distressing situation at her uncle's house and, quite understandably, has forgotten to have an explanation ready, Burney lectures: 'Foresight . . . made no part of the character of Camilla, whose impetuous disposition was open to every danger of indiscretion' (216). Every single imprudence of Camilla's, such as her walking around a strange town with Mrs Mittin, is made to produce the worst conceivable consequences. Burney so structured the novel that Camilla's, Lionel's and Clermont Lynmere's debts hit the Tyrold family at the same time; hence Camilla's excusable errors are associated with the culpable ones of the young men, so that their guilt seems to spread to her. It is specifically Camilla's debt, not theirs, that sends her venerated father to debtors' prison. Burney, like Mrs Tyrold, seems to be treating most severely the child she loves most.

Burney's explicit statements about her moral purpose as a novelist do not support the theory that she was consciously subverting the conventional code. In the Dedication to *The Wanderer*, she justifies novels on moral grounds in the following terms: a book's fiction enwraps 'illustrations of conduct, that the most rigid preceptor need not deem dangerous to entrust to his pupils; . . . to make pleasant the path of propriety, is snatching from evil its most alluring mode of ascendency' (xxii). She dedicated *Camilla* to Queen Charlotte, a highly conventional woman whom she loved and respected, recommending it on the grounds that the Queen delighted 'in all ways to speed the progress of Morality' (3). She would hardly have done so unless she had in mind morality that the Queen would have approved.

When she gratuitously introduced a reprehension of Hester Thrale Piozzi into her *Memoirs of Dr. Burney* (1832), years after Hester's marriage and death, she manifested a narrow morality and self-righteousness fully worthy of Mrs Tyrold. She marvels that a woman of Hester's social station, distinguished education and high origin could sink into 'the witlessly impetuous tribe, who immolate fame, interest, and duty to the shrine of passion'; she endorses Dr Burney's outrage at Hester's dereliction from (imaginary) maternal duty; and she concludes by pluming herself on her consistency in refusing to congratulate Hester after her marriage. She adds that both she and her father eagerly waited 'for any opportunity that might re-open so dear a friendship, without warring against their principles, or disturbing their reverence for truth' (2:387–91).

The internal contradictions in *Camilla* may result from

Burney's deep emotional involvement with her material; she drew on her own intense personal relationships and, in Camilla herself, may have been looking back at her own outgrown girlish self, heightening both faults and misfortunes for fictional effect. Her emphasis on Camilla's imagination (constantly mentioned, though never demonstrated) suggests that she may have been chastising her own indulgence in imaginative activity through the fictional character.

The connection between Burney's situation at the time of writing and the views she was expressing is problematic. It seems incongruous that she would write a novel preaching female repression at a time when she was joyously fulfilled – happily married, with an infant son. Doody uses this as evidence that she must have been attacking the conventional repressive rules, since she had just attained happiness by breaking them: that is, making advances to d'Arblay, letting her feelings show, and disregarding her father's advice (*Burney* 230). On the other hand, Hemlow suggests that her unconventional marriage made it necessary for her to prove her propriety in the novel, especially as she needed the Queen's support (249–50). The Blooms argue that Burney's tranquil fulfillment prevented *Camilla* from being a subversive (or imaginatively vital) novel, for she 'needed to be pulled by an inner tension . . . between a fairy tale world she envisioned for herself and the frustrations or uncertainties with which she lived' (231).

All we can conclude is that conflicting impulses in Burney produced conflicting signals in *Camilla*. She may have meant to suggest that Camilla should not have followed her father's advice and that she is unfairly blamed on the basis of misguided and perfectionist standards. If so, however, the distinction between Camilla's view and the author's should have been made clearer. It would have been possible to indicate delicately that an intelligent and well-meaning parental figure may give bad advice that should not be followed, as Austen did with Lady Russell and Anne Elliot in *Persuasion* (1818). When Camilla accuses herself of reprehensible thoughtlessness for occasioning a duel, Burney may have meant to suggest that she is misguided by using the words 'she felt . . . seemed . . . appeared.' But Burney never clearly dissociated her moral views from Camilla's. There is no question that Huck Finn was meant to show a good heart and a deformed conscience; one cannot be so sure about Camilla.

IV

Protest Against the World's Law

WHATEVER THE INTERPRETATIONS Burney intended for specific characters, she developed one conflict in *Camilla* quite clearly and openly: that between legalistic morality, associated with reason, and spontaneous goodness, associated with imagination. Camilla's difficulties result from the fact that she is spontaneously good, while those who direct her conscience see virtue only in law and principle. Burney insists on the importance of such virtue, but she reveals its tendency to be judgmental, rigid and puritanical. To Eugenia, the most perfect example of Tyrold morality, 'That to which she was most unwilling, appeared, to the strictness of her principles, to be most proper' (314). Through Sir Hugh and Mrs Arlbery, Burney presents an alternative to this kind of virtue – kindness and good will, following rather than repressing nature and unconcerned with judgment. They appreciate Camilla for what she is; unfortunately for her, the world, represented by the people she most reveres, demands from young women, above all, correct behavior.

By describing her amiable heroine as impulsive and intense, Burney revealed her attraction to emotional freedom; by censuring her for it, Burney asserted her commitment to the conventional feminine ideal and the belief that law and principle are the only reliable guides to conduct. She is warmly attached to Camilla, but she praises her sister Lavinia, whose only characteristic is blamelessness. Throughout the book, Burney contrasts characters who are impulsively good with those who maintain virtue by following law and duty and distrust spontaneity on principle. The second group avoids mistakes and is explicitly praised; the first is more attractive and spreads more happiness, but is not presented as awesomely virtuous.

Actually, the novel seems to dissociate goodness and kindness from virtue and reason, since none of the characters has both sets of qualities. Sir Hugh's determination to think the best of everybody is associated with his stupidity; Mrs Arlbery's lack of interest in judging people, with her levity. Camilla and Sir Hugh, who have the best hearts in the book (according to the servant Jacob, 573), act from impulse rather than principle and are constantly criticized for imprudence. Camilla is distinguished for sweetness, eagerness to make other people happy, charitable abstention from censure and loving gratitude – none of which qualities are conspicuous in Edgar or the Tyrold parents. She lacks their ability to act according to principle, control personal feelings and calculate consequences prudently. Edgar, disapproving of Mrs Arlbery, makes Camilla give up her first dinner invitation on the grounds that Sir Hugh was not asked beforehand; actually, we soon find out, Sir Hugh would not think of hesitating to approve whatever 'could give her any pleasure' (109).

Sir Hugh remarks, when he learns that the Edgar–Camilla marriage has collapsed, as well as the marriages he had planned: 'now I've seen a little more of the world, I can't say I find much difference between the good and the bad, with respect to their all doing alike' (774). It looks like another example of his inability to think clearly, but actually his statement is proved true by the events of the plot, where 'good' people contribute no more, perhaps less, to others' happiness than 'bad' ones do. In a book that constantly preaches the importance of obeying the law, it is an astonishingly subversive statement; for it brings into question the whole rationale for repressive morality based on the innate sinfulness of human nature. Why should people immolate themselves to duty when this produces no benefit to anyone?

The highly articulate Mrs Arlbery can make this point more convincingly than Sir Hugh. Her free spirit is particularly refreshing in this novel where practically everyone is a slave to duty. She is a woman of character, but in every other respect represents what people like Edgar dislike and distrust in women – she uses rouge and practises coquetry, she defies convention and public opinion, she pays no tribute to virtue or self-control, and she laughs at men. Nevertheless, although she flouts the explicit moral teaching of the novel, she is not only attractive but nice, not only witty but penetrating, not only good-humored but good-hearted.

Arlbery's unabashed self-indulgence does not hurt anyone, and thus belies the Tyrold belief that self-repression is inherently a moral virtue. In fact, self-repression seems to generate unhappiness in others as well as oneself. Mrs Tyrold never gives pleasure to anyone, especially not to the children she loves so much. It is true that Arlbery will not spend time with people who bore her – but why should she? She constantly makes it evident that she does not care what people think of her, yet (unlike Lionel) she does not hurt people, because the feelings and opinions she disregards are not in fact important. Burney makes a nice distinction between women who intelligently calculate their rebellion against repressive control and those who mindlessly pursue unrestricted freedom, like Miss Dennel.

Arlbery appears to be right when she assures Camilla that wits like herself 'have often as good hearts . . . as the careful prosers who utter nothing but what is right, or the heavy thinkers who have too little fancy to say anything that is wrong' (780). Although she does not practice systematic charity like the Tyrolds, she is usually ready to help people in need; and her efforts may be more effective than their more orthodox ones, as when she helps to get off a poor prisoner by charming his lawyer to exert himself (96), an effort to which a woman like Mrs Tyrold would never stoop. Her character suggests the moral advantages of freedom, for she has a free-flowing good will not evident in more conspicuously virtuous characters, whether it is evidenced by her extending her hospitality to Sir Hugh's servants and his horses (which he can appreciate, unlike the more highly principled senior Tyrolds, 206) or by her immediately forgiving a slight from Camilla when she sees how unhappy she is (778). She is one of the few characters who tries to encourage Camilla and cheer her up, though her motive is not principle but a dislike of long faces.

Arlbery's light approach can suddenly open up the virtuous unrelieved earnestness of the Tyrolds. Mr Tyrold's dark warnings of 'the world's' condemnation of a woman who reveals unrequited love seems persuasive in its context. But then Burney shows how casually Arlbery and her equally worldly friend Sir Sedley Clarendel recognize the source of Camilla's unhappiness, and we see how absurd his fears are outside the self-conscious Tyrold world. Moreover, the two worldlings immediately start planning practical measures to help her, while all her parents can do is enjoin stern self-repression. Edgar helps Camilla only by watching her censoriously and loading her with advice which does not keep her out of any trouble; Clarendel saves her life. Burney artfully unfolds Clarendel's character, revealing that an apparent selfish fop may have capacities for love and courage and showing him developing altruistic concern as his idle flirtation with Camilla turns into a love that almost reconciles him to marriage.

The contrast between their two world views is neatly brought out when Camilla suffers agonies of remorse for having encouraged Clarendel by flirting with him in order to make Edgar jealous and by involuntarily accepting a loan from him. She consults desperately with her sisters on how to extricate herself from her involvement with him; she realizes she has unwittingly led him on, and they all agonize over his wounded heart and her jeopardized honor. At last she nerves herself to go and explain herself – and, at the first hint that she does not love him, he pretends he never had any serious interest in her. The whole problem evaporates when the situation is seen in proportion. It is perfectly in character for him to subordinate his genuine affection to his need to preserve his self-esteem as a man too sophisticated to love without requital. It is also an ironic commentary on the unnecessary moral scruples and tortured conscience produced by an overly serious view of life. Completely unaware of the 'principle' that motivated her, her guilt over leading him on and supposedly making him suffer, he cannot imagine why she came to meet him if she loved Edgar instead.

Although she is constricted by the discipline she has learned, Camilla is naturally inclined to emotional excess, manifested in impulsiveness, enthusiasm, intense moods, passionate feelings, thinking controlled by desire rather than logic. Burney, confusingly, calls this tendency 'imagination': the 'reigning and radical defect' of Camilla's character is 'an imagination that submitted to no control.' It also, however, contributes to her attractiveness: 'it caught, by its force and fire, the quick-kindling admiration of the lively; it possessed, by magnetic pervasion, the witchery to create sympathy in the most serious' (84).

The term 'imagination' in Burney's novels does not refer to the creative faculty, but seems to be equivalent to 'sensibility'. This is evident from the character of Mrs Berlinton, whose reckless behavior – she reacts to a loveless marriage by flirting with many men and carrying on an impassioned friendship with one – is attributed to a susceptible heart, romantic sentiments and an exalted imagination (487). Her imagination misleads her into believing that a platonic love-affair is possible. Camilla's stubborn attachment to Berlinton is hard to understand in literal terms, since her charm is not demonstrated and her cultivation of a passionate extramarital friendship is shockingly immoral by Camilla's standards. Berlinton appeals to her because she represents the extreme of emotional susceptibility, to which Camilla is dangerously attracted, and she symbolically works out the passionate indulgence that Burney could never allow to her heroine. By making her only eighteen, close to Camilla's age, Burney underlined their similarity and suggested Camilla's potential for making the same errors.

Because any kind of release for women aroused sexual fears, *imagination* took on sexual implications. It was also an acceptable substitute term for the sexual susceptibility that could not be acknowledged in virtuous women. Cecilia controls her love for Delvile by keeping busy, 'that her heart might have less leisure for imagination'; that is, for indulgence in desire (251; Spacks, 'Ev'ry Woman' 41–2). Alerting Evelina against yielding to her unrecognized passion for Lord Orville, which she must not indulge because it does not seem likely to be ratified by marriage, Villars tells her: '*imagination* took the reins,' leaving surer-footed *reason* behind; this 'new guide' rapidly led her through the 'regions of fancy and passion' until, unawares, she fell in love (308). The young philosopher Eugenia suppressed her attraction to Melmond because she considered herself already engaged, for she 'denied her imagination any power over her reason' (116). Understood as relaxation of rational control over sexual feelings, imagination provokes guilt, anxiety and a sense of peril. This extended use of *imagination* also reflects Burney's ambivalence about her writing, as she translates her own guilt about creative expression into her heroine's guilt about sexual expression, a guilt to which all women are liable. Charlotte Perkins Gilman was to make a similar intuitive connection between imagination and rebellion against societal control in 'The Yellow Wallpaper' (1892), where the heroine's rational, authoritarian husband tries to suppress her imaginative activity and it therefore turns into a frightening, disruptive force.

By definition opposed to rational control, imagination has

direct moral implications when the dominant morality is one of rational law. Camilla could not repress her love for Edgar, even when it seemed hopeless, and constantly let her feelings overwhelm her ability to think things through, whether she thoughtlessly led on Hal Westwyn to make Edgar jealous (680) or merely put off hearing distressing news (154). When she was overcome with guilt because her debts sent her father to prison, she wished to die and made herself ill by doing without food and rest. But 'Conscience now suddenly took the reins from the hands of imagination,' she remembered the duties and principles that her despondent feelings had obscured, and she realized that suicide would be egotistical and cruel to those who loved her (872). Unlike reason, sensibility cannot be a reliable moral guide: it is a 'delicate, but irregular power, which now impels to all that is most disinterested for others, now forgets all mankind, to watch the pulsations of its own fancies' (680). Since Camilla could not be accused of selfish obliviousness to others' feelings (like other heroines of sensibility such as Marianne Dashwood), the threatened danger seems to be letting herself be controlled by emotion instead of reason.

Reason in *Camilla* is generally invoked to enforce conformity. It regulates the impulses and fantasies that express individual desire and enforces truth as defined by the consensus of social opinion. Most people would agree with Mr Tyrold that it is reasonable to adjust to reality – but reality tends to be defined by existing conditions. In the male-dominated society of the eighteenth century, a social hierarchy dominated by men and sharply distinguished spheres based on a pervasive 'sexual character' were assumed to reflect the order of nature. Even those who would not go so far as Gregory – who claimed that 'The love of dress' is 'natural' to women and therefore is 'proper and reasonable' (55–6) – assumed that modesty, timidity and compliance were innate in the female character. A woman who aspired to be reasonable would have to shape her behavior accordingly. The neoclassical assumption that the general opinion was more apt to be right than that of any individual further discouraged any deviating conception of reality.

Thus Hannah More could turn women's reason into an internalized restrictive force:

> The more a woman's understanding is improved, the more obviously she will discern that there can be no happiness in any society where there is a perpetual struggle for power; and the more her judgment is rectified, the more accurate views will she take of the station she was born to fill, and the more readily will she accommodate to it. (2:14)

Providence has 'obviously marked out' a 'plain path' for women, she went on, and 'custom has for the most part rationally confirmed them' in it (2:14, 22). Maria Edgeworth would appeal to a girl's reason to convince her that 'the delicacy and reserve of female manners' 'are indispensably connected with the largest interests of society, and with [her] highest pleasures' (*Letters* 61–2). Burke wrote that people 'have no right to what is not reasonable, and to what is not for their benefit' (74). Even Wollstonecraft stated that 'to submit to reason is to submit to the nature of things, and to that God, who formed them so, to promote our real interest' (*Vindication* 271). Thus, whether reason liberates or imposes limits depends on one's interpretation of the station woman was born to fill, of what rights are reasonable and beneficial, of what is the nature of things. If the natural order was deduced from existing society, as conservatives deduced it, reason dictated subordination of women to men and denial of any rights that would encourage women to be bold or self-assertive.

Reason directs one to act morally ('he that thinks reasonably must think morally,' as Johnson wrote in his 'Preface to Shakespeare'), but law and principle supported the established status quo: things were as they were because God, as well as nature, ordained them so. Morality was defined by the ruling class to support its own position. Accordingly, women were enjoined to subordinate their interests to those of the male-headed family, to control their emotions, to respect convention and established order. Feelings that supported the hierarchical order – deference to convention, pride in wealth and social position – were defined as rational; those that threatened it, notably sexual love, were condemned as passion. In fact, many eighteenth-century women, including Burney herself, could be emboldened only by love to defy patriarchal authority; this may have been why novels, which typically endorsed the rights of love, were morally condemned, especially for women.

Hester Thrale acutely formulated the dilemma of reasonable women when she argued with herself about marrying Gabriel Piozzi:

> I married the first Time to please my Mother, I must marry the second Time to please my Daughter – I have always sacrificed my own Choice to that of others, so I must sacrifice it again: – but why? Oh because I am a Woman of superior Understanding, & must not for the World degrade my self from my Situation in Life. but if I *have* superior Understanding, let me at least make use of it for once; & rise to the Rank of a human Being conscious of its own power to discern Good from Ill – the person who has uniformly acted by the Will of others, has hardly that Dignity to boast. (545)

Thrale's friends, including Burney, accepted the first side of her argument and rejected the rebuttal. Woman's reason was to be used not in thinking for herself but in controlling herself. When women were praised for being more rational than men, the meaning was always that they were better able to control their impulses, as when Burney defended Thrale by insisting that she struggled against her love for Piozzi rather than yielding to 'male and headstrong passion' (*Memoirs* 2:246). In her last appeal to Thrale to dissuade her from marrying Piozzi (January 1783), Burney warned her: 'The Mother of 5 Children, 3 of them as Tall as herself, will never be forgiven for shewing so great an ascendance of passion over Reason.' How, she asks, can Thrale sacrifice everything – '*Children* – *Religion, Friends/Country, Character*' – for a hope of happiness 'so uncertain! so *inadequate* to such a sacrifice . . . a gratification that no one can *esteem*, not even he for whom you feel it' (qtd Doody, *Burney* 162). Burney, although a genuinely sympathetic friend, here accepts her society's reversal of reason and senseless prejudice: it seems to her unreasonable for a woman to marry a man because she loves him, because she is acting from passion; reasonable to ostracize such a woman for seeking her own happiness, because she is opposing conventional practice and values.[28]

All the respectable authorities in *Camilla* use reason to support their conventional views. Mrs Tyrold, who is so conspicuously clear-sighted in her understanding of situations and consequences, is directed by her reason to subject her intelligence and energy to orthodox duty and patriarchal order. The arguments of Mr Tyrold's letter proceed by clear logical steps, and he appeals to Camilla's good sense to conquer her feelings and remind her of the importance of conformity. With sound logic and obliviousness to the natural operations of feeling, he tells her that she must reveal neither tenderness nor reserve toward Edgar, because he has neither proposed nor done anything to offend her (360).

Edgar is a thorough rationalist, made anxious by falling in love, because love 'enwraps the imagination, and masters the reason!' (233). He is expert at enlisting reason to promote his ends, whether to justify his wishes or to rationalize his unseemly passions. He is displeased to see that Camilla is enjoying herself and being admired at a party, because he wants her confined to 'the rational serenity of domestic life' (706). When he resolves to renounce her rather than tolerate jealousy on her account (provoked by her graciousness to Major Cerwood), he claims to be motivated not by sexual outrage, but by high principle: 'Am I capable of love without trust? . . . No! I will not be such a slave to the delusions of inclination. I will abandon neither my honour nor my judgment to my wishes' (292). In his own mind, Edgar justifies his perpetual testing of Camilla as establishing 'the perfect confidence, and unbounded esteem' one should have for a wife (725). Richardson's Lovelace used the same rationalization.

If reason was used to enforce self-repression and conformity, women whose self-respect depended on being reasonable could not escape from conventional limitations. Every Burney heroine knows from the beginning or soon learns that she must control her impulses and fit herself into a socially ordained role. This submission is dictated by morality, but also by rational acceptance of social and natural reality. The only escape was to defy reasonableness. Burney included in each of her novels a free spirit, always a woman, who defies convention and offers an alternative to the proper, self-controlled model provided by the heroine. Burney protected the moral tendency of her work by criticizing these characters – but she also endowed them with attractive qualities and did not punish them for their deviations. They are too bold to be exemplary, but they are nevertheless clear-sighted and on the whole sympathetically treated.

While Mrs Selwyn of *Evelina* deviates from feminine propriety, her successors, more interestingly, deviate from the orthodox reason that supported it. Lady Honoria Pemberton of *Cecilia* unblushingly flouts the standards of rational responsibility. The episode in which she insists to Delvile and Cecilia that she is safest standing under a tree during a thunderstorm is elaborately set up to show the dangerous ignorance of a woman who refuses to cultivate her reason. The moral implications are shown by her flippant repetition of scandalous stories without the least concern for supporting evidence, for which Mrs Delvile gravely rebukes her. 'She had quick parts and high spirits, though her mind was uncultivated, and she was totally void of judgment or discretion: she was careless of giving offence, and indifferent to all that was thought of her' (464).

There is a significant contrast, however, between Honoria and a brainless character like Larolles, although both have a flow of words that does not proceed along the lines of logical discourse.[29] Honoria never professes emotions that she does not feel, while Larolles gushes with sympathy and affection that she does not even realize are false. While Larolles runs on, oblivious to the fact that she is contradicting herself every other sentence, Honoria's speeches make sense although her lively mind does not build logical arguments. She rejoices that the inane Lord Derford is coming to relieve the gravity of Delvile Castle:

> We can ask him . . . for a little news, and that will put Mrs. Delvile in a passion, which will help to give us a little spirit: though I know we shall not get the smallest intelligence from him, for he knows nothing in the world that's going forward. And indeed, that's no great matter, for if he did, he would not know how to tell it, he's so excessively silly. (465)

Although each statement literally contradicts the one before it, they add up to prove her point that Derford will, one way or another, provide her with amusement.

Honoria's disregard for rational order in argument naturally extends to playful questioning of the social order that was supposed to be based on reason. She wonders that Cecilia does not want to marry Derford, 'for you might have done exactly what you pleased with him.' When Cecilia declares with propriety that she would rather marry a tutor than a pupil, Honoria replies, 'I am sure I should not . . . for one has enough to do with tutors before hand. . . . I fancy you think so too, only it's a pretty speech to make' (465–6). This is not what a young lady should say, and it does not conform to eighteenth-century ideas of rational social order; but it raises the possibility that Cecilia's consistently correct views owe as much to her pride in propriety as to her rational evaluations. Honoria gravely suggests that, when Mortimer comes into his estate, he should make Delvile

Castle useful by a simple alteration: 'only . . . take out these old windows, and fix some thick iron grates in their place, and so turn the castle into a gaol for the county' (505). This not only makes fun of old Delvile's family pride, but expresses the symbolic truth that the inhabitants of the castle are imprisoned by traditional beliefs. This is the point in the story when young Delvile resolves to tear himself away from Cecilia, even though he loves her, because he believes that changing his name to marry her would degrade his honor and his family. He is sacrificing his 'love, happiness, and inclination' (and hers, although he does not know it) to what he calls 'duty, spirit, and fortitude' (513).

Mrs Delvile rightly censures Honoria's tendency to laugh 'at whatever goes forward' (497), but in Burney's world of constraints, frustrations, duty and guilt, it is a welcome relief. We can understand why Honoria hates dignity (935) when we recall that women were often required to maintain their dignity by repressing their most intense feelings. It is one of her pranks that brings the lovers together by precipitating Delvile's declaration of love to Cecilia and proposal of (secret) marriage, when he overhears Cecilia expressing her love for him to his dog, which Honoria has had sent to her.

After Cecilia has married Delvile and settled into his home, Honoria enlivens the solemn atmosphere with her irresponsible freedom. She playfully suggests the advantages of conjugal discord: 'while you are quarrelling you may say any thing, and demand any thing, but when you are reconciled, you ought to behave pretty, and seem contented.' To Cecilia's comment that these principles might alarm her suitors, Honoria shrewdly replies that 'not a creature thinks of our principles, till they find them out by our conduct' after marriage. 'The men know nothing of us in the world while we are single, but how we can dance a minuet, or play a lesson upon the harpsichord' (934–5). She has figured out a practicable way of surviving in an unfair system.

Honoria infuriates old Delvile when she remarks, very truly, that Cecilia has made a bad bargain, for nobody 'cares for the noble blood of the Delviles but themselves,' while everybody cares for a fortune. 'What should we all do with birth if it was not for wealth? it would neither take us to Ranelagh nor the Opera; nor buy us caps, nor wigs, nor supply us with dinners, nor bouquets' (936–7). Honoria has neatly deflated three platitudes that were used to keep women in order: that there could be no conflict of wills in a harmonious marriage, that women attracted men by their meritorious character and that money was less important than breeding. She recognizes that upper-class status is based on money. Her irrationality frees her from conventional thinking as well as logic and opens an escape from dutiful submission to restrictive reality.

In the same way, Mrs Arlbery's flighty speeches may shock conventional thinking, but they often prove to be right. To Honoria's fresh originality, she adds intellectual and moral weight. Arlbery demonstrates her acuity by being the only person in the novel to see through Edgar Mandlebert. She understands, as the virtuously wise people do not, that Edgar's constant critical attention to Camilla indicates that he wishes to marry her (420); and she also recognizes his tendency to torment her, remarking on his lack of 'generosity to act openly' (461). Finally, she draws a grim and accurate picture of what he will be like as a husband:

> You do not see, he does not, perhaps, himself know, how exactly he is calculated to make you wretched. He is a watcher; and a watcher, restless and perturbed himself, infests all he pursues with uneasiness. He is without trust, and therefore without either courage or consistency. To-day he may be persuaded you will make all his happiness; to-morrow, he may fear you will give him nothing but misery. Yet it is not that he is jealous of any other; 'tis of the object of his choice he is jealous, lest she should not prove good enough to merit it.

She points to Edgar's selfishness in hesitating to commit himself to Camilla and his hypocrisy in considering it consistent with honor to maintain his own freedom while engaging her affections and keeping her from any other connection, so long as he does not actually propose. She sees his demand for single-minded affection for the Lovelace-type egotism it is: 'the egotism of looking out for something that is wholly devoted to them, and that has not a breath to breathe that is not a sigh for their perfections' (482–4).

Attacking Edgar entails attacking the judiciousness, good conduct and adherence to principle that he undoubtedly displays. The only way to do this is to ridicule the reason that rightly maintains that these are admirable qualities. Arlbery does not hesitate to do so:

> That Mandlebert . . . is my aversion. He has just that air and reputation of faultlessness that gives me the spleen. I hope, for her sake, he won't think of her; he will lead her a terrible life. A man who piques himself upon his perfections, finds no mode so convenient and ready for displaying them, as proving all about him to be constantly in the wrong.

Proposing that Sir Sedley Clarendel cure Camilla by courting her himself, she compares the two men: 'In conversation, too, you are nearly upon a par, for he is as regularly too right, as you are ridiculously too wrong, – but O the charm of dear amusing wrong, over dull commanding right!' (367)

Clarendel, an anticipation of a Wildean dandy, specializes in outrageous nonsense with an edge of truth, as in his 'Papas and mamas . . . are ever most egregiously in the way' (263). Doody has called attention to the chess game in which he flaunts his lack of attention to the game as he is checkmated (249; *Burney* 235–6). Like the rules of chess, the larger rules of custom, which others take so seriously, may often be disregarded with impunity. Burney lets Arlbery sense that 'right,' as defined by her society, limits and deadens by confining thought to logical connections, goodness to the following of rational rules. Burney seems to be hinting at a connection between conventional reasonableness and the patriarchal order when she has Clarendel playfully justify not keeping a bargain on the grounds that thinking 'of the same scheme two days together' is absurdly 'patriarchal' (400).

When Arlbery calls Edgar 'too right,' she is conceding to the world's definition of wisdom. However, both she and her author recognize that there is another sort of truth. She playfully, but accurately, claims that her apparent capriciousness is not the opposite of philosophy: 'I, like the sage, though not with sage-like motives, save time that must otherwise be wasted; brave rules that would murder common sense; and when I have made people stare, turn another way that I may laugh' (246). Burney shared many of Arlbery's opinions about foolish people and senseless customs, and Arlbery says many things that Burney would have liked to say in her own person. But Burney could only express her carefree playfulness in a familiar supportive environment such as Chessington. Her report of a conversation there in which she developed the contents of a mock Treatise upon Politeness (*ED* 1:324–8) shows exactly the same type of humor as Arlbery's on the advantages of a regiment's moving on (252). In making Arlbery echo the address to herself as Nobody that opened her diary – Arlbery 'could not be so accommodating as to perform Nobody under her own roof' (259) – Burney suggests an opposition but also an association between character and author.[30]

Arlbery's capricious and dictatorial treatment of men appears perverse, but it turns out to have a purpose. Flouting the conduct books, she tells Camilla not to comply or worry about male displeasure. 'Men, my dear, are all spoilt by humility, and all conquered by gaiety. . . . From the instant you permit them to think of being offended, they become your masters; and you will find it vastly more convenient to make them your slaves'

124

(446–7). Burney's novels show Arlbery to be right. While the proper women are consistently oppressed and exploited by men, Arlbery generally gets them to do what she wants. She keeps them fascinated by professing indifference to them – never for a moment acknowledging superiority in them or dependency in herself.

In the same way, she puts public opinion – that terror of women – into its proper perspective. Her public demeanor pointedly illustrates 'that confident ease, that unabashed countenance, which seems to set the company at defiance' against which Gregory warned his daughters (29–30). She explains the shrewd policy behind it:

> You are made a slave in a moment by the world, if you don't begin life by defying it. Take your own way, follow your own humour, and you and the world will both go on just as well, as if you ask its will and pleasure for everything you do, and want, and think. (246)

Nothing in the novel proves her wrong. She does what women were direly warned against and gets away with it. The only consequence of her flouting public opinion is shocking people like Edgar, which does not matter to her; she is accepted, even courted, by everyone she likes. (Similarly, the mannish Mrs Selwyn of *Evelina* is said to have made herself universally disliked by her sarcastic tongue; but Burney shows her thoroughly enjoying herself in society.)

It could be argued that Arlbery is more reasonable than people like Mrs Tyrold, because she critically examines customs and traditional attitudes and rejects them if she finds them senseless. That was the position of contemporary radicals, and of Thrale when she resolved to marry Piozzi. But Burney preferred to present Arlbery's truth as a feminine alternative to reason, lightening it further by caprice and levity.

Although she lived her life according to reason and law,

Burney was attracted to women of imagination and undisciplined good feeling. She loved and admired Mrs Thrale and Madame de Staël, but regretted that both were more impulsive, passionate and imprudent than seemed properly feminine. She fervently admired de Staël's 'bewitching' good heart and generosity, as well as her intellect, but lamented her lack of 'principles' and 'unrestrained passions' (*DL* 1:406; *Fanny Burney and the Burneys* 94).

Many women of her time shared her ambivalent attitude. The rise of sentimentalism valorized feelings for everyone, but women were more restricted than men by laws they had not made. Not only radical writers like Wollstonecraft and Inchbald, but relatively conservative ones like Burney and Austen, presented the claims of free-flowing imagination; and all associated it with emotional warmth and sexual desire. In Elizabeth Hamilton's *Memoirs of Modern Philosophers* (1800), exemplary Harriet Orwell is warned against letting her imagination delude her reason into yielding to a passion she could otherwise resist, namely her love for a young man who has not enough money to marry her. The idealistic but tragically misguided Julia, in the same novel, is misled by her imagination to elope with a revolutionary; she is striving for a more flamboyant virtue than that of ordinary Christianity, and she learns that women should sensibly limit their aspirations. Emily St Aubert's warm sensibility adds to her charm, but her father rightly sees the need to discipline it by teaching her rational self-command (Radcliffe, *The Mysteries of Udolpho* [1794] 5).

Hannah More seems to have had Camilla's and Julia's distinguishing quality in mind when she warned that 'a warm, tender, disinterested, and enthusiastic spirit' was the quality most apt 'to endanger the peace and to expose the virtue of its possessor'; in such a character, 'the judgment is little exercised, the reasoning powers are seldom brought into action, and self-knowledge and self-denial scarcely included' (2:96–8, 102). More liberal writers took a positive view of the same quality. Frances Brooke's Maria of *The Excursion* (1779), an author aspiring to fame as well as an ardent, unguarded lover, is allowed exceptional imprudence for a heroine headed for a happy ending; Brooke makes clear that Maria's generosity and enthusiasm amply compensate for her ignoring of propriety. Mrs Glenmorris, the wise mother in Charlotte Smith's *The Young Philosopher* (1798), would not like her daughter's 'imagination to outrun her reason' to the point of causing her to live in a fantasy world, but she wishes her to be 'romantically' capable of unreserved friendship, independent thinking and naturalness:

> . . . if affection for merit, if admiration of talents, if the attachments of friendship are romantic; if it be romantic to dare to have an opinion of one's own, and not to follow one formal tract, whether wrong or right, pleasant or irksome, because our grandmothers and aunts have followed it before . . . oh! may my Medora still be the child of nature and simplicity, still venture to express all she feels, even at the risk of being called a strange romantic girl. (2:14–15)

In varying proportions, all these women were attracted to imaginative and emotional freedom while committed to the need for rational limitation. Burney occupied a moderate position, between More's stern warning and Smith's only slightly reserved enthusiasm. Unfortunately, as Tompkins has pointed out, scarcely any of these free-spirited heroines are persuasively developed (169). Most, like Camilla, are not convincingly imprudent.

The only women writers who successfully worked out the conflicting claims of spontaneous goodness and legalistic morality, imaginative freedom and salutary good sense, were Inchbald, in the first part of *A Simple Story* (1791), and Austen, in *Sense and Sensibility* (1811). Unlike her contemporaries, Inchbald was willing to present a seriously flawed heroine, whose errors bring her to a tragic conclusion. Miss Milner really is imprudent and impulsive. Warm, spontaneous and generous, she is also unreasonable and unwilling to resist doing whatever she feels like doing. It is typical of her that she risks losing the man she loves by attending a masquerade against his orders, simply to assert her independence. The hero, Dorriforth, a rationally controlled, absolutely upright man, also has the faults of his virtues: he has repudiated the child of his once-beloved dead sister because she married out of their religion. Milner could not banish someone for an offence; he could not violate his principles. She errs but forgives freely; he neither errs nor forgives. Inchbald's characters are placed in meaningful opposition, and her attitudes toward them are clear. She openly despises the blameless Miss Fenton, who can be a model of feminine propriety because she lacks any warm feelings to control. She suggests that good feeling might be a safer moral guide than principle by showing how even conscientious, rational people like the priest Sandford may mistake their own motives (123–4). She openly questions the assumption that law is the only foundation for goodness and presents sympathetically a heroine who actually sins.

Austen presents a more positive view of law in *Sense and Sensibility*, for she contrasts her heroine of sensibility with a normative heroine who combines warmth with self-control, intelligence with decorum. Although Austen's ideological position was close to Burney's, she defines her theme in a more satisfying way: she displays unmistakably both the errors produced by disregard of the world's law and the faults produced by excessive respect for it. Unlike Camilla, the lovable Marianne really does err through imprudence, overactive imagination and the slighting of law in favor of feeling. On the other side, in characters like the John Dashwoods, Austen shows prudence degenerating into mean calculation and cold pursuit of self-interest. Finally, Austen comes to a coherent resolution of the issue that Burney leaves ambiguous and confused: Marianne realizes her errors and settles for limited happiness.

V

THE WANDERER: A Political Analysis of the World

IN HER LAST NOVEL, *The Wanderer: or, Female Difficulties*, Burney returned to consider woman's position in the larger society, as she had in *Cecilia*, but in a more far-reaching and analytical way. Stimulated by the upheaval of the French Revolution, she directed attention to problems that could not be solved by personal adjustment or reform; she touched on all social levels, rather than confining herself to the genteel upper class; and she probed causes more deeply. At the time she published *Camilla*, Burney primly remarked that politics was 'not a *feminine* subject for discussion' (*JL* 3:186), but in *The Wanderer*, although she still disavowed overt concern with politics, she acknowledged that the Revolution was 'blended . . . with every intellectual survey of the present times' (xviii–xix). She ridiculed the view that women cannot understand politics by making a particularly dull male character ask her intelligent heroine whether any gentlemen of her family were with her 'in foreign parts,' so that he can hear something about current affairs in France; he means no offense, he assures her, because 'inferiority of understanding' is 'no defect in a female' (83).

A conservatice character in *The Wanderer* describes the psychological impact of the Revolution: 'Its undistinguishing admirers, it has emancipated from all rule and order; while its unwilling, yet observant and suffering witnesses, have been formed by it to fortitude, prudence, and philosophy' (833). Elinor Joddrel, Burney's anti-heroine, represents the first group; Juliet Granville, her heroine, the second. But, although the immediate cause of Juliet's sufferings is her loss of social and financial position as a result of the Revolution, her experience illustrates the enduring problems of women in Burney's own patriarchal society. And, although Elinor is inspired by uncritical enthusiasm for the French Revolution, she voices telling attacks upon the English system. Through Elinor, Burney explicitly brings a political dimension to her presentation of female difficulties. Even though she dissociates herself from Elinor's feminist analysis, she uses the character to raise the issues, seriously considers her views, and takes pains to answer them with reasoned argument.

By making her heroine a fugitive from the Reign of Terror, Burney isolates her from normal social supports. As a penniless political exile, Juliet has no family, no friends, no social status, no means of support, no recognized identity. Because she has had to disguise herself by dressing in rags, hiding her face and darkening her skin, she lacks even the beauty and genteel appearance that brought women limited consideration. Burney reduces her heroine to 'unaccommodated woman,' the better to expose the precariousness of woman's position in her supposedly civilized Christian society, where no one was respected without extrinsic advantages that women could rarely command for themselves. As the book opens, Juliet is desperately begging for a place on a small boat headed for England; in a foretaste of the picture of society that will be presented, the unhesitating reaction of the respectable passengers is to ignore her, and then, after two men insist on taking her in, to shun or bait her.

The society that was empty-headed and unfeeling in *Cecilia* is malicious and cruel in *The Wanderer*. Juliet is deserving and needy, and almost everyone she meets ignores her deserts and assumes that her need makes her contemptible. The male protectors who were supposed to safeguard women in patriarchal society, irresponsible in *Cecilia* and misguided in *Camilla*, are not even present in *The Wanderer* – until Juliet's legal protector appears near the end of the book. He is a brute whom she has been forced to marry and who comes to claim her as his legal property (Cutting, 'Defiant Women: The Growth of Feminism in Fanny Burney's Novels' 528). Yet the fiction remains that social institutions have been set up to take care of women.

One of the few people to help Juliet, the old Admiral who insisted on taking her into the boat, unwittingly underlines this point as he maintains the conventional rationale in the teeth of the evidence. He is himself a genuinely chivalrous and responsible member of the ruling class, accepting the obligation to help a defenseless woman and condemning men who seduce and abandon women. On the other hand, he assumes without any evidence except Juliet's solitary state that this must be her situation: 'the devil himself never yet put it into a man's head, nor into the world's neither, to abandon . . . a woman who has kept tight to her own duty, and taken a modest care of herself' (28). This complacent view is belied by the very situation in which they are: Mrs Maple, Mrs Ireton, Mr Ireton and Mr Riley would not extend help to a needy woman, however virtuous she might be. Juliet's experience bears out Wollstonecraft's observation, 'I have seldom seen much compassion excited by the helplessness of females, unless they were fair; then, perhaps, pity was the soft hand-maid of love, or the harbinger of lust' (*Vindication* 262). Because she is aware of this motivation, Juliet feels she must reject help from Harleigh, the only person reliably willing and able to help her.

The Admiral illustrates the pernicious effects of patriarchal ideology more clearly than a figure like old Mr Delvile, because in the former case Burney shows how ideology can counteract a kindly nature. His kindness cannot extend to helping Juliet to escape from her dreadful husband. He will not condone 'a wife in running away from her lawful spouse,' regardless of the circumstances (807). A woman may not even indulge in relief at hearing of her bad husband's death: 'a husband's a husband; and I don't much uphold a wife's not thinking of that; for, if a woman may mutiny against her husband, there's an end to all discipline' (820). The Admiral would not think of hurting a woman himself, but he condemns out of hand one who runs away from an abusive husband, for his principles force him to value patriarchal law above individual feeling. Burney suggests a connection between his male chauvinism and his national prejudice against the French. He is convinced of male and British superiority, but, since he is incapable of rational thought, he merely states prejudices without any attempt to support them by reason. There is a final delicious touch when Harleigh asks his and the French Bishop's consent to his marrying Juliet (the Bishop is her foster-father; the Admiral turns out to be her uncle). The wise Bishop consents because he trusts Juliet's judgment; the thick-headed Admiral, because he knows a weak female needs a husband to guide her (828).[31]

By isolating the heroine from family and friends, Burney avoids complications from personal relationships and focuses on the conflict between the female individual and society. Juliet is constrained not so much by faulty individuals as by social institutions and group attitudes that evaluate her only on extrinsic circumstances. Without wealth or social position, without male protection, without friends or even a name, Juliet's extraordinary personal talents, strength and virtue cannot help her to make her way in society or even to be respected, even though she is intelligent, musically gifted and charming, and has profited from the best of lady's educations.

Her strength is remarkable, considering that nothing in that education has prepared her to stand on her own: as a lady, she has been brought up expecting to be supported by her family. Nevertheless, she is firmly resolved to support herself now that this has become necessary. She manages to keep up her courage through setback after setback; she resolutely accepts unpalatable choices, usually of humiliating dependency, when, after rational consideration, she sees the alternative would be even worse. She has more self-confidence than the earlier heroines, so that she generally feels sure that she has made the right choice, and does not believe herself responsible when things go wrong. If people uncharitably misjudge her, she may excuse them because she recognizes that appearances are against her; but she does not accept the misjudgments as a reflection upon herself. Juliet does not require reassurance and guidance, only the opportunity to use her abilities and efforts to support herself. She fervently hopes to exchange her 'helpless dependancy,' for 'an honorable, however fatiguing, exertion of the talents and acquirements with which she has been endowed by her education' (197). This is as emphatic as Wollstonecraft's declaration, 'Independence I have long considered as the grand blessing of life, the basis of every virtue; and independence I will ever secure by contracting my wants, though I were to live on a barren heath' (*Vindication* 85).[32]

But Burney did not share Wollstonecraft's confidence that a woman can gain independence, if only she is resolute enough. And probably, for most women, Burney's evaluation was the more realistic. Juliet discovers that the jobs open to the best qualified lady are few, low-paid, precarious and demeaning. The lack of economic opportunities for women was recognized as an acute social problem in the later eighteenth century, addressed in detail by Wollstonecraft, Hays, Edgeworth, Mary Ann Radcliffe (*The Female Advocate*, 1799) and Priscilla Wakefield (*Reflections on the Present Condition of the Female Sex*, 1798). But *The Wanderer* is one of the few novels of the period that seriously considers work. Burney drew on the experience of her relatives to examine the trials of a private music teacher. She describes in detail the operation of a milliner's shop, the lack of consideration on the part of customers and the dishonest tricks of salespeople. Despite her sympathy with the difficulties of working people, Burney does not sentimentalize them; they too are keenly responsive to class – nothing is too much for rich customers or too little for poor ones (404–6). Since *The Wanderer* is told from the viewpoint of a genteel woman struggling for survival, it arouses more lively involvement with her plight than the tracts and can reveal more insight into her attitude toward work, both the psychological barriers that add to her difficulties and the benefits that can be obtained.

For, although Burney displays her sensitive heroine swallowing mortifications, overburdened by routine labor and offended by commercial chicanery, she does not stop there. She recognizes that work has psychological as well as economic value, neither of which was available to ladies. Juliet takes an interest in the business of a farm where she is staying because she realizes that lack of occupation 'was a principal cause . . . of female difficulties' (664). Earlier, work has roused her from the self-pity and lethargy produced by slights and isolation: 'Her spirits, from the fullness of her occupations, revived; and she soon grew a stranger to the depression of that ruminating leisure, which is wasted in regret, in repining, or in wavering meditation' (224; Epstein 185).

Burney's main emphasis, however, is on Juliet's troubles, which she generalizes by calling them 'Female Difficulties' – a phrase that is the subtitle of the novel and is recalled at four strategic points within it (257, 377, 664, 836). It is true that calling these difficulties 'female' suggests some inherent weakness in women; but both content and context show that they are caused by social attitudes and conditions. Facing the collapse of her plan to support herself by giving private harp lessons, Juliet exclaims to herself:

> . . . how insufficient . . . is a FEMALE to herself! How utterly dependant upon situation – connexions – circumstance! how nameless, how for ever fresh-springing are her DIFFICULTIES, when she would owe her existence to her own exertions! Her

conduct is criticised, not scrutinized; her character is censured, not examined; her labours are unhonoured, and her qualifications are but lures to ill will! (257)

Women were insufficient to themselves only because society insisted upon judging them not by what they did but by what was said about them; this made them dependent on men or older women for the respectability that could only come from position in a family, and vulnerable to the attacks of whoever influenced public opinion. Because modesty was supposed to keep women from seeking distinction of any kind, one who put herself forward in any way laid herself open to uncharitable judgments, which in turn blighted her attempts to gain recognition.

Juliet finds that the demands of public opinion are even more of an obstacle to her search for employment than her lack of training and opportunities. Some jobs were arbitrarily defined as disreputable, while others were closed to those whose reputations were not considered impeccable. The first type a lady could not take unless she was prepared to sacrifice what she had been brought up to value most, social approval assuring her secure place in genteel society. The second type she could not get unless she was well thought of by those influential in local society, who judged her by her situation, without bothering to investigate her character and conduct.

Because Juliet has no visible connections, she cannot get the job most obviously suitable for her, that of governess. She can give private harp lessons only because one of the harridans who run local society finds it convenient to recommend her. When it becomes known that she is friendless, the social leaders scent some kind of impropriety, and that is enough to make them withdraw their daughters from her tutelage. She is advised to establish herself as a professional teacher by giving a public concert, in which case her reputation will not matter. The catch here is that public performers were considered to have no reputations to lose, so that she would be giving up her status as a lady. It is not pride but her need for social survival that inhibits Juliet from public paid performance:

> . . . my pride, on the contrary, urges me to every exertion that may lead to self-dependence: but who is permitted to act by the sole guidance of their own perceptions and notions? who is so free, – I might better, perhaps, say so desolate, – as to consider themselves clear of all responsibility to the opinions of others? (276)

Pride and self-respect, which should work together, are pitted against each other – the one urging self-reliant achievement, the other depending on the good opinion of others who would condemn any public efforts. Freedom from such narrow opinions seems desirable, but its price is an isolation that is even worse than constraint.

Juliet's trepidations about publicly performing for pay are confirmed by the reactions of other characters, which she is right to take seriously because her situation does in fact depend upon others' opinions. As soon as she agrees to become professional, the young ladies who are performing as amateurs go out of their way to distinguish themselves from her (293). Harleigh passionately warns her that she risks blighting her prospects of union with an upper-class family, such as his own; although he could overlook it, his relatives would not. This is deeply upsetting to Juliet, because her ultimate position and her own self-respect depend upon retaining the esteem of such people. Of all the jobs she tries, this is the only one that would bring her good money, as well as prestige, satisfaction and independence – and this is the one that would destroy her status as a lady (Simons 106).

Juliet tries to make her living by sewing, in the wistful hope that she can thereby combine respectability with 'self-dependence' (429); but she finds that there is not enough piecework for the multitude of young women who need it. So at last she is forced to accept a job as companion to Mrs Ireton. This is so excessively demeaning – her employer insults her continually and regards any preference on her part as a presumption – that no self-respecting human being can stand it. Juliet is expected to be on duty all the time, to be constantly cheerful and entertaining, 'prating, or holding her tongue; doing every thing she was bid; and keeping always on hand' (464). Her labor is not only unremitting but unrewarded: 'Success . . . was unacknowledged, though failure was resented' (469). Juliet soon finds that success is not even attainable: since Mrs Ireton cannot be satisfied with anything long and cannot bear to see a dependent settled and comfortable, the only pleasure that lasts for her is visibly to exert power over others, and soon Juliet can only amuse her by being a butt 'for the exercise of tyranny and caprice' (468).

Simons points to the irony that this paid companion position is both Juliet's most humiliating and unpleasant job and the one most acceptable to society (104). That is because it could not possibly threaten woman's traditional role, for it offered no gratification and it reinforced dependence and compliance. Indeed, it was very close to what women were expected to do in their families without being paid – to be constantly on hand to cheer, support and put up with their relatives, regardless of whether they were as disagreeable as Mrs Ireton. Burney's sympathetic presentation of Juliet's situation shows her wisely reconsidering her uncharitable presentation of Miss Bennet, the paid companion of Monckton's wife in *Cecilia*. She had dismissed Bennet as a natural toady, as if she had chosen to attain 'affluence without labour' by being dependent on a disagreeable woman, did not mind being 'a slave of the mistress of the house' and 'the tool of it's master,' and therefore deserved to be treated with indignity (11).

With her usual resolution and positive thinking, Juliet has managed to reason herself into believing that, however unpleasant it was to be Mrs Ireton's companion, it was not degrading as long as she avoided sycophancy, by not flattering her, and parasitism, by giving value for money in the form of pleasing and serving. She credits this philosophical attitude to Giles Arbe, a kindly eccentric whose oddity enables him to see through conventional attitudes (466). Then, by a cutting irony, she finds that this philosophy is beyond his scope. All he can see is that a paid companion accepts a salary to conceal her thoughts, repress her desires, beg pardon when she is not at fault and take abuse from a child and a dog; he does not hesitate to equate this employment with selling her integrity for money (497). He charitably hopes that Juliet has not so demeaned herself – but his charity does not extend to understanding that circumstances may force self-respecting people to swallow insults, and that such people deserve sympathy rather than scorn. Kindly Arbe is no more capable of imagining himself in a situation that could not be his than is judgmental Marchmont, who condemned women forced to marry for financial support. Both men see mercenary behaviour; neither troubles himself to look for the compulsion behind it.

Burney concludes her book with a peroration on female difficulties:

> Here, and thus felicitously, ended, with the acknowledgement of her name, and her family, the DIFFICULTIES of the WANDERER; – a being who had been cast upon herself; a female Robinson Crusoe, as unaided and unprotected, though in the midst of the world, as that imaginary hero in his un-inhabited island; . . .
> How mighty, thus circumstanced, are the DIFFICULTIES with which a FEMALE has to struggle! Her honour always in danger of being assailed, her delicacy of being offended, her strength of being exhausted, and her virtue of being calumniated! Yet even DIFFICULTIES such as these are not insurmountable, where mental courage, operating through patience, prudence, and principle, supply physical force, combat disappointment, and keep the untamed spirits superiour to failure, and ever alive to hope. (836)

The sentimental emphasis produced by the capitalization and the difficulties listed is counteracted by the reference to Robinson Crusoe. For, by comparing Juliet's unsupported state to Crusoe's isolation on his island, Burney invites us to contrast male preparation for life with female incapacitation. Like Crusoe, Juliet must either starve or find resources to support herself; but, while everything in his training has developed resourcefulness, enterprise, self-reliance and initiative, everything in Juliet's has been designed to render her helpless and dependent. Even when she can manage to get remunerative work, she must worry whether her present or future family might consider it improper; and she must also contend against her own impulses to shrink from self-promotion and vulgar associations.

It is this socially-induced pressure, rather than innate female debility, that causes her to collapse as she walks toward the stage to perform at her concert. Her determined efforts to be resolute and enterprising are constantly undermined by her fears that they are unfeminine. She has to fight her socialization as a lady in order to do anything to help herself. Whereas Cecilia was constrained mostly by external forces, Burney's more sophisticated analysis of social influence in *The Wanderer* shows Juliet rendered powerless by her own inhibitions as well. Her reluctance or even incapacity to put herself forward, to be suspected with a man, to risk losing social approval, to take violent or forceful action, constrain her just as surely as the lack of business opportunities. The elegant circumlocutions of Burney's late style appropriately convey the inhibitions of the character and perhaps of her author as well.

The advice of actual eighteenth-century moralists confirms that Juliet's inhibitions are not a fictional exaggeration. Edgeworth, a relatively liberal writer, illustrates the debilitating effects of the prudence that was inculcated in women. Starting from the assumption that girls 'cannot rectify' any 'material mistakes in their conduct,' she recommends 'Timidity, a certain tardiness of decision, and reluctance to act in public situations' to keep them secure. A woman's 'pausing prudence'

> does not to a man of discernment denote imbecility, but appears to him the graceful auspicious characteristic of female virtue. There is always more probability, that women should endanger their own happiness by precipitation, than by for-bearance. Promptitude of choice is seldom expected from the female sex; . . . We should even in trifles avoid every circum-stance which can tend to make girls venturesome, which can encourage them to trust to their good fortune, instead of relying on their own prudence. (*Practical Education* 699–700)

The inhibitions produced by this sort of teaching could sap women's confidence to the point of disabling them to make decisions and take action.

A woman was made to feel that it was unfeminine and un-ladylike to assert herself, to make claims, to make herself publicly conspicuous, to attack her own problems rather than looking to a male protector. When Burney made her heroic journey to join her injured husband in Trèves, she took care to conceal her identity; for she knew he would be mortified to have it known that his wife traveled alone, without ceremony or even adequate money (*JL* 8:494). Because it was expected that ladies did not support themselves, they took paid work only as the result of a fall in status, and therefore working itself was seen as a degradation (Wollstonecraft, *Vindication* 261). Burney was embarrassed to receive a salary even from the Queen: 'I can never take possession of [money] without a se-cret feeling of something like a degradation' (*DL* 3:142). Both Smith and Inchbald, two of her most gifted contemporaries, felt it necessary to declare that they had become novelists by necessity rather than choice (Prefaces to *Desmond* [1792] and *A Simple Story* [1791]). Edgeworth confirms that: 'There is no employment, at present, by which a gentlewoman can main-tain herself without losing something of [her] rank in society'

(*Education* 548). And yet it was essential for a lady to retain her genteel status, because she had been brought up to base her self-respect upon it.

Juliet's frustrated attempts to be judged on her own merits, rather than by other people's interpretation of appearances, bring to a focus one of Burney's major preoccupations in her life and her fiction: the awful power of public opinion, especially over women, and the irresponsible and capricious way it is formed. A woman's possibilities for employment, for marriage, for social acceptance and freedom from insult all depended on her reputation. Theoretically, no one would doubt a woman's virtue if she behaved with total correctness, as the Admiral declared. Actually, a woman was judged according to the people she was connected with and the impressions strangers formed of her, even if they were ill-informed, narrow-minded, or spiteful.

Juliet is perpetually being misjudged, despite her totally virtuous character and unfailingly correct behaviour, because of chance and the habits and prejudices of women who are highly placed although personally contemptible. She must deny herself sensible and desirable options – performing in public, accepting money from Harleigh – because they might lead to misconstruction. And yet she is still so suspect because of circumstances she cannot control that she is subject to insult and barred from genteel employment. She was accepted in local society because she happened to be living with Mrs Maple, who happened to find it convenient to produce her as a guest, which made it necessary to present her as a lady; she was rejected when young Ireton casually revealed that she had appeared from nowhere, shabbily dressed.

Women could not control the appearances by which people judged them, nor could they take positive action to counterbalance unfavorable appearances. Jean-Jacques Rousseau laid this out explicitly:

> A man . . . secure in his own good conduct, depends only on
> himself, and may brave the public opinion: but a woman, in
> behaving well, performs but half her duty; as what is thought
> of her, is as important to her as what she really is. (qtd Woll-
> stonecraft, *Vindication* 242)

This widely held opinion reinforced women's tendency to be
timid and passive, since the surest way to avoid blame is to do
nothing. Burney herself once explained that she protected herself from repentance by running from risks and abstaining
from action (*DL* 3:392).

Even while she recognized that public opinion was often
senseless, she feared to disregard it. She involved herself in
comic contortions to avoid conversing with women of question-
able reputation, while at the same time avoiding unladylike
plain-speaking. She and Germaine de Staël had been charmed
with each other when they met, but then Dr Burney revealed
that de Staël had 'been accused of partiality to M. de Narbonne.'
From then on, Frances kept backing away from de Staël, who
could not understand what had happened. She was very upset
when de Staël innocently called at the Burney home – what
would people think? Even after her marriage, the d'Arblays
spent time agonizing over what to do when de Staël tried yet
again to be friends. On another occasion, when Burney was
traveling by stagecoach, she was agitated to discover that one
of her fellow passengers was an actress. Some actresses, she
knew, were perfectly respectable – but what if this one was
not? How dreadful to discover such a thing after voluntarily
speaking to her! At last she found a happy solution: she busied
herself with some children she was escorting, so she did not
have to talk at all (*JL* 2:20, 34; 5:234–5). Characteristically, she
protected her purity by restricting herself.

Yet Burney did occasionally allow herself to chafe at such
restrictions. She complained after giving up Madame de Staël:
'I wish The World would take more care of itself, and less of its
neighbours . . . there seemed an absolute resolution formed to

crush this acquaintance, & compel me to appear its wilful renouncer' (*JL* 2:123). The compulsion was more galling because she was put in the position of willing her own submission, as Cecilia had been by Mrs Delvile. Even when Burney was conforming to the stultifying decorum of the Court, she inwardly retained an independence of judgment inconceivable to her colleagues. She remarked about one of the gentlemen there, 'How people are always living for others, or rather not living at all, lest others should think they live unwisely!' (*DL* 3:502). Mrs Arlbery could not have been more emphatic.[33]

Burney's novels demonstrate the same ambivalence. In *Cecilia*, she cast doubt on the worth of public opinion when she remarked that the villain Monckton was well accepted in society because he observed the forms. The same public voice that severely condemns anyone whose behavior or situation deviates from what is normally expected blandly accepts those who scrupulously defer to convention without inquiring into their morals (8). In *Camilla*, she explicitly condemned people's tendency to make uncharitable judgments based on inadequate evidence, but laid heavier emphasis on the imprudence of opening opportunities for such misjudgments. In *The Wanderer*, it is decidedly the judges who are at fault, rather than the judged. Even there, however, Burney suggests a connection between aspersion and guilt. When Juliet is upset by being seen with a rake, even though she has done everything humanly possible to avoid him, the narrator half-blames her: 'For with however just a pride wronged innocence may disdain injurious aspersions, female fame, like the wife of Caesar, ought never to be suspected' (454).

Nevertheless, in this book, Burney lays bare the basis of the world's judgment, and shows that it is not only misguided but culpably frivolous. For the first time, she places her main emphasis on the malicious irresponsibility of those who misjudge people without due cause. They do not even pretend to have a rational basis for their misjudgments. They disdain poverty, recoil from misfortune, and are uncomfortable about anything out of the ordinary; and they justify their suspicions to themselves by identifying these conditions with bad character. Their proneness to censure is often based on insecurity. A person like Mrs Maple has no basis for self-esteem except being well thought of by her peers, and no way of securing their good opinion except by denigrating those who do not fit the group's standards. Having no intrinsic good qualities, she can only establish her moral status by averting criticism from herself; the readiest way to do so is to adhere fanatically to convention.

She is forced to answer crude Mr Riley, who is baiting her about taking Elinor to France, because, 'however unwilling [she was] to hold a public conference with a person of whom she had never seen the pedigree, nor the rent-roll,' she 'could still less endure to let even a shadow of blame against herself pass unanswered' (232). She alternates between grudgingly patronizing Juliet, to prevent the world from suspecting that she could have countenanced anyone who was not a lady, and vilifying her, to prevent a suspicion that she could have patronized an 'adventurer.' She actually feels guilt for having made it possible for Juliet to be favored by the best people, and she quiets her conscience 'by devoutly resolving, that no entreaties . . . should ever in future, dupe her out of her own good sense, into other people's fantastical conceits of charity' (196). Thus Burney shows how rigid conventionality, misidentified as good sense, both encourages and justifies narrow uncharitableness.

In Lady Kendover, the highest-ranking woman in the world of *The Wanderer*, Burney offers a devastating comment on the leadership of public opinion. Lady Kendover does not even have the excuse of insecurity; she simply cannot be bothered to investigate any individual case. It is easier to base her judgments on prejudice or general opinion. And yet, because the world's slavishness ensures that her judgment will be respected because of her rank, she can destroy people's social standing and means of livelihood. She will patronize only artists who have already come into notice through patronage: 'to draw forth talents from obscurity, to honour indigent virtue, were exertions that demanded a character of a superiour species; a character that had learnt to act for himself, by thinking for himself and feeling for others' (214). It is this nonentity who is responsible for the community's decision (made after they have demonstrated their correctness by cutting Juliet at church)

> that it was utterly impossible to admit a young woman, so obscurely involved in strange circumstances, and so ready to fall into low company [a farmer, a steward and a rich grocer], to so confidential a kind of intercourse, as that of giving instructions to young persons of fashion. (256)

The vagueness of the charge is significant. Lady Kendover does not have to say what is immoral about talking with a grocer; just implying something wrong is enough to make others feel it would be prudent to avoid Juliet.

It is women who lead public opinion in the mean little society of *The Wanderer*.[34] In this book Burney develops more fully than before the ways in which a patriarchal society distorts women's characters so that they comply with their oppression. Women's enforced preoccupation with their own reputation increased their concern with that of others and led them to become the strongest guardians of the female morality and propriety to which they had sacrificed themselves. Even gentle Mary Delany, who had preserved a clear conscience by sacrificing her youth to an odious marriage demanded by her family, declared that separation discredited a wife regardless of the circumstances; the resultant taint would even blight her daughters' chances for marriage: 'who will venture on the daughter, when the mother has proved such a wife!' (1:91–2). Moreover, with little opportunity for positive achievement, women could display virtue by policing other women. Hannah More even defined women's main contribution to society as enforcing the ostracism of adulterous wives (1:46–9). Men could rely on women to uphold the conventions, because, as the subordinate group, they were discouraged from thinking for themselves, made to feel insecure unless that had the approval of men, and fearful of losing that approval if they did not conform to male expectations. As a privileged subgroup, respectable upper-class women protected their own position by insisting on convention more than men felt the need to do.

The connection between oppressive female authority and patriarchal society is most obvious in the case of Mrs Ireton, the most odious woman in the book. She is a product of the false masculine values that overestimate women with beauty and depreciate women without it. A beauty in her youth, she became accustomed to having everyone applaud her wit and sensibility and thus developed inflated self-esteem and the expectation of constant attention. In middle age, she continues to play off the same airs, but to no effect. She persists because she cannot accept the fact that any admiration she could attract vanished with her beauty, but she is sufficiently aware of her decline that she has become bitter and nasty (517–18). Now everyone but herself can see that what passed for wit in her youth is heavy sarcasm devoid of anything but the will to abuse. No longer able to influence men through charm, she can find satisfaction only in exerting the power of money by hurting her financial dependents.

Although callous and irresponsible wielders of power were nothing new in Burney's fiction, her presentation of power and privilege in *The Wanderer* evinces a new class consciousness. Instead of singling out unworthy individuals, as she had in *Evelina* and even *Cecilia*, she suggests that classes of people get power for arbitrary reasons and wield it capriciously, and that class privilege in itself is apt to harden the heart. In the opening scene in the boat, before any character has been identified, she sets out a stark contrast between those who have privilege and those who have not, and indicates how few of the first group are willing to share.

For the first time, Burney writes from the viewpoint of an outcast, one who depends for survival on the good feeling of the upper class. Through Juliet, she constantly calls attention to the problems of groups without power, especially poor working people. Juliet learns that 'mental freedom' is illusory without financial security and that employers' demands are insatiable: when she starts out working as hard as she can to make a good impression, she finds that she has only succeeded in setting herself an impossibly high standard that she is thenceforth expected to meet (429–31, 451). Members of the privileged class withhold money as casually as they destroy reputations. Ingenuous Giles Arbe cannot understand why the parents of Juliet's music students have not paid her: she answers that it is their 'want of knowing . . . the value of a little to the self-supported and distressed! The want, in short, of consideration' (274). Only Mr Tedman, the *nouveau riche* grocer, whom the genteel characters sneer at, not only pays what he owes her, but notices her need and pays her in advance; his careful counting of pennies lays him open to ridicule, but it looks very good compared to upper-class obliviousness to the needs of those not born rich (283).

Burney's empathy even moves her to raise a doubt about the moral quality of the genteel code by which her heroine lives. When Juliet primly refuses money from Giles Arbe on the grounds that she does not incur obligations to strange men, he questions the pride that does not prevent her from, in effect, taking money from the tradespeople she cannot pay, who need their money far more than he does; and she has no answer (262–3). This issue is never resolved, but it remains a disturbing critique of the assumption that a lady's delicacy is more important than other people's needs.

When Juliet comes to work for Mrs Ireton, she finds her

surrounded by unhappy dependents. She is bullying a black slave, a nursery maid, a salesman who is trying to do business with her and a charity child who has been sent to collect the maintenance that Mrs Ireton has promised but neglected to send. Her authority is equally, though more subtly, damaging to the two dependents she spoils, an overfed dog and an undisciplined little boy. Burney's sympathetic picture of society's underdogs is quite inclusive.

Burney used Juliet's detachment from her normal social setting to take her through all levels of society. While the earlier heroines were embarrassed by overbearing attentiveness from men at parties, Juliet, working as a shop assistant, finds herself on permanent display to the stares of the idle young men of the neighborhood. Sir Lyell Sycamore, reacting to her apparent social inferiority, hardly bothers to court her; and she can escape his pressing attentions only by taking service with Mrs Ireton. Later, like any poor woman although unlike a novel heroine, Juliet must travel across country alone and on foot. She is constantly being accosted; and, as she gets tired and begins to walk slowly, looking around eagerly for a place to rest, she is assumed to be trying to pick up a man. To laborers returning weary from their morning's work she seems 'exactly fashioned' to provide a refreshing diversion. Everyone who passes makes some remark, a coarse compliment or a solicitation for a kiss (640). Finally a couple of louts decide it would be a bit of fun to rape her, and she only escapes through exceptional presence of mind and luck.

Burney even brings Juliet to board on a farm so she can observe the oppression of women there, which is simply a coarser version of what they endure in the upper and middle class. The farmer considers women inferior because they cannot plough or mow; his contempt is mitigated only by his recognition that they are the mothers of men. Although he did not mistreat his wife and daughters, he 'considered them as his servants: and when they were diligent and useful, he praised them and gave them presents; and, when their work was done, suffered them to seek what diversion they pleased, without interference or controul.' As old Mr Delvile reverenced his son as his successor (462), the farmer shares his authority and profits with his sons, who domineer over their sisters and mother (666). Despite being so emphatically a lady, Juliet can see the connection between her own situation and that of shopgirls or farmers' daughters. She finds that women of every class are devalued and forced into passivity. This was remarkable in the eighteenth-century women's novel, for even the radicals wrote about lady heroines, whose problems were chiefly emotional; Mary Wollstonecraft's Maria is a colorless heroine in the refined sentimental tradition, whose harrowing problems do not include making her own living.[35]

Although Burney bravely asserts that mental courage can overcome inhibitions, prejudices and other female difficulties, her book demonstrates the contrary. Juliet's own efforts get her the companion job with Mrs Ireton that no amount of positive thinking can render tolerable. By herself, she cannot attain wealth or social position or the respect that goes with them. In the end she is saved by Harleigh's extraordinarily persistent devotion and her family's decision to recognize her. The fairy-tale ending is effective in *The Wanderer*, for it contrasts so glaringly with the grim realism used to detail Juliet's practical problems in making her living that it seems intended to draw attention to them rather than to offer a pretended solution (Cutting, 'Defiant Women' 529–30).[36] Burney raises the question of what happens to deserving women who do not have selflessly devoted suitors and secret aristocratic connections, and pointedly leaves it open.

Her character Elinor, on the other hand, offers a clear solution to the intractable problems raised by Juliet's situation: women must liberate themselves by throwing off traditional restrictions. Elinor rejects the easy assumption of Mr Tyrold and Dr Gregory that contemporary custom and nature are one, although she does realize that it is hard to separate them: custom is a tyrant that 'awes our very nature itself, and bewilders and confounds even our free will! We are slaves to its laws and its follies, till we forget its usurpation' (160). She rationally demolishes the conventional assumption that propriety requires women to be passive, pointing out the natural right 'of woman, if endowed with senses, to make use of them' (162). Far from increasing feminine dignity, abstention from expressing and acting on her feelings degrades a woman into an automaton: is it more high-minded for her to choose a man because he merits her love or merely to bestow her affections 'as the recompence of flattery received?' 'Must she be taught to subdue all [her heart's] native emotions? To hide them as sin, and to deny them as shame?' (163) Burney lets her character explicitly challenge conventional morality, rather than indirectly undercutting it through a discordance between statement and plot, as she had in *Camilla*.

However, Elinor's cogent reasoning is itself undercut by its context. She voices her theories in a scene that she has set up in order to confront Harleigh with her declaration of love. She is in a state of manic elation, controlled by her passions at the very time she is insisting on her rationality. She denies the weakness of trying to work on Harleigh's compassion when that is exactly what she is doing. She invokes theoretical systems to support her personal position and needs; her powerful argument that forcing passivity upon women degrades them is undercut by the fact that she is using it as a justification for love suicide. Even if it were not a crime on religious grounds, suicide is not rationally defensible for her because it is not warranted by her situation. Her choice of love object, as well as her method of courting him, is further evidence of her poor judgment, since he is a man for whom sweetness, softness, dignity and delicacy are essential virtues in a woman (174). Elinor reveals self-centeredness as well as mental instability, for she is doing her best to spread her unhappiness to innocent parties: she is trying to make Harleigh feel guilty and is grossly inconsiderate of Juliet.

Burney used Elinor to express her own protest against conventional restrictions on women, to respond to the theories of contemporary radical feminists Mary Wollstonecraft and Mary Hays, and to indicate what was wrong with their position. She let Elinor argue with insight and truth and endowed her with noble and attractive qualities, but she also made clear that Elinor is impractical, self-deluded, self-indulgent and self-destructive. Burney could not imagine freedom, at least female freedom, that was not dangerously out of control.

Elinor is so intoxicated with theory that she is not aware of practical realities. Having a comfortable income of her own and therefore no contact with the working world, she cannot see Juliet's difficulties in earning her living. Committed to honest expression of her own feelings as a matter of principle, she accuses anyone not so outspoken of lukewarmness or hypocrisy (as does Austen's Marianne). Elinor shows unfairness to Juliet, as well as obliviousness to the real world, when she reproaches her for prudence and caution. 'You . . . and such as you . . . act always by rule . . . never utter a word of which you have not weighed the consequence; never indulge a wish of which you have not canvassed the effects: . . . listen to no generous feeling; . . . shrink from every liberal impulse' (560). She mistakes control of impulse for lack of feeling, and she ignores what would have happened to Juliet had she not been cautious. Conservatives like Burney and Juliet recognized that forces other than reason inevitably governed social life, and had to be reckoned with. As Edgeworth put it, women's happiness 'is of more consequence than their speculative rights; and we wish to educate women so that they may be happy in the situations in which they are most likely to be placed' (*Education* 168). Elinor loses the man she loves by her disregard of rules and consequences, and would have fared still worse had she not enjoyed fortune and a secure social position.

Elinor refuses to look at the practical difficulties of Juliet's situation. When Juliet laments 'the severe DIFFICULTIES of a FEMALE, who, without fortune or protection, had her way to make in the world,' Elinor derides her 'Debility and folly' and exhorts her to stop thinking of herself as 'a dawdling woman'; if she will remember that she is 'an active human being,' her 'FEMALE DIFFICULTIES' will 'vanish into the vapour of which they are formed'. 'Misery,' Elinor boasts, 'has taught me to conquer mine!' (377) Elinor's argument that female difficulties are artificially created is very reasonable, but, as usual, she ignores actual circumstances. No one can fulfill her potential independent of society. Juliet has had to face genuine external difficulties, from lack of useful training to narrow prejudice, and even such internal feelings as shrinking from public display cannot be casually thrown off. Self-reliance is not so easily attained in a patriarchal society as Elinor believes. She can speak confidently only because she has never had to deal with Juliet's problems; her own, of course, are irrelevant because they *are* self-generated. At the time of this conversation, she is recovering from a wound, self-inflicted because she cannot have her way in love; Juliet has taken valuable time from work she has to do in order to visit her (Doody, *Burney* 349–50).

Nevertheless, Elinor raises searching questions about the conventional limitations on women's activity. She charges that Juliet only fears 'to alarm, or offend the men – who would keep us from every office, but making puddings and pies for their own precious palates!' (378). The echo from brutal Captain Mirvan (*Evelina* 109) indicates Burney's sympathy with Elinor's opinion. Elinor goes on to quote the arguments used by Hays and Wollstonecraft: that men reduce women to insignificance and then attribute this to nature; that 'They dare not trust us with their own education, and their own opportunities for distinction'; that there is no basis for equating women's inferior bodily strength with inferiority in understanding (378–9).

The Wanderer: a political analysis of the world

Like Hays in her *Appeal to the Men of Great Britain in Behalf of Women* (1798), Elinor exposes the inconsistency which disparages woman while expecting her to be better than man:

> They require from her, in defiance of their examples! – in defiance of their lures! – angelical perfection. She must be mistress of her passions; she must never listen to her inclinations; . . . she must not pursue a measure of which she cannot publish the motive; she must always be guided by reason, though they deny her understanding! – Frankness, the noblest of our qualities, is her disgrace; – sympathy, the most exquisite of our feelings, is her bane! (379)

Elinor protests the damaging assumptions, ambiguously treated in *Camilla*, that reason in woman consists of suppressing her desires and that it is possible for her to combine artless openness about her motives with discreet control of her speech.

By demonstrating that women cannot depend on men or society for support, the plot of *The Wanderer* proves Elinor's contention that women must develop independence. Too conservative to approve of her refusal to be governed by opinions she has not examined and prejudices she does not agree with, Burney nevertheless shows her virtuous heroine victimized by just such opinions and prejudices. Elinor's contempt for unthinking conformity is substantiated by characters like Mrs Maple, whose narrow lack of sympathy is justified by a stupid conventionality that rejects anything out of the ordinary as improper. Clearly, Elinor is morally as well as intellectually superior. Unlike the female slaves to convention, narrow in their sympathies, willing to sacrifice truth and their own feelings in order to maintain a respectable appearance, and too eager to escape blame ever to admit themselves in the wrong, she is generous, superior to artifice, and eager to compensate when convinced of error. She does, in fact, compare favorably with every other woman in the book except the heroine and her cousin Lady Aurora (one of Burney's blank blameless women).

Elinor is even given the chance to criticize the exemplary conservative Albert Harleigh. Probably, she says, he does not yet know his own feelings, for while he has considered her 'as the property of his brother, his pride is so scrupulous, and his scruples are so squeamish, that he would deem it a crime of the first magnitude' to wonder, even to himself, whether he would like Elinor for himself. This is a perverse distortion of Harleigh's fastidious honor, but it is cleverly phrased; for the word 'property' recalls the men in *Cecilia* who denied a woman the right to dispose of herself and suggests that legalistic morality considers property law more sacred than love. She goes on to challenge his respect for tradition:

> He is suspicious of some sophistry in whatever is not established by antiquated rules; . . . he is constantly anxious not to offend that conceited old prejudice, that thinks it taking a liberty with human nature, to suppose that any man can be so indecent as to grow up wiser, or more knowing, than his grandpapa was before him. (147)

This skillfully reduces to absurdity Edmund Burke's dire warnings against innovation in *Reflections on the Revolution in France* (1790), which were based on the assumptions that human nature is unchanging and that institutions and even prejudices survive the test of time because they embody wisdom.

Burney had always sympathized with those who defied convention to judge for themselves, from her stepsister in her early diary to Belfield in *Cecilia*, although she could not approve of them. *Cecilia* opens with a debate on conformity, in which Belfield exclaims against the ideology that teaches man 'that he must neither consult his understanding, nor pursue his inclinations, lest . . . his understanding should provoke him to despise [fools]; and his inclinations . . . give him courage to abjure . . . the tyranny of perpetual restraint' (15).

Although Belfield will show himself to be undisciplined and impractical, he is also represented as intelligent and idealistic.[37] By expressing such feelings so persuasively, by attributing them to characters in many ways admirable, Burney revealed her awareness and resentment of the constraints that she felt obliged to impose upon herself.

While Burney could not approve of Elinor's breaking her engagement with Dennis Harleigh because she fell in love with Albert, she lets her raise an awkward issue by declaring that it would have been 'despicable' to have married Dennis 'from mere cowardly conformity' when she adored his brother (141). For Burney's own life suggests, and her novels confirm, that it *is* despicable to marry a man one does not care for. When other novelists considered this problem of a woman's having second thoughts about her engagement, they usually evaded the issue by getting rid of the undesired fiancé, as Charlotte Smith did for her Emmeline.

Elinor's account of her broken engagement displays her frankness, her readiness to flout propriety, and great acuity. She happened to meet Dennis, a young lawyer, who discussed his cases with her. 'I always took the opposite side to that which he was employed to plead, in order to try his powers, and prove my own.' They moved on to debate on the French Revolution and the Rights of Man. 'He had fallen desperately in love with me, either for my wit or my fortune, or both; and therefore all topics were sure to be approved.' She delighted in a 'warfare' in which she 'was certain to be always victorious':

> . . . the joy I experienced in the display of my own talents, made me doat upon his sight. The truth is, our mutual vanity mutually deceived us: he saw my pleasure in his company, and concluded that it was personal regard: I found nothing to rouse the energies of my faculties in his absence, and imagined myself enamoured of my vanquished antagonist. (139)

The mutual attraction between Elinor and Dennis, plausible

despite their lack of real congeniality, is acutely analyzed; and in letting Elinor analyze it herself, Burney provides evidence of her wit and honesty, as well as her ability to laugh at herself. Elinor is too intelligent, however, to be permanently taken in by appeals to her vanity: one reason she turned from Dennis to Albert, Albert explains, is that 'her disdain of flattery, or even of civil acquiescence,' made her prefer his frank criticism of her opinions to 'the courteous complaisance which my brother deemed due to his situation of her humble servant' (566).

Elinor goes on to justify her passion for Albert, which caused her to break off her scheduled marriage and to pursue him – equally scandalous acts in eighteenth-century eyes. At the same time that Burney makes her reveal her dangerous lack of self-control through her incoherent manner, she lets her eloquently voice the romantic aspiration for something finer than ordinary life. Elinor argues that we should liberate ourselves through passion, which is 'all that snatches us from mere inert existence' and which leads us to 'our noblest conceptions of all that is towering and sublime.' With this 'mental enlargement', she says,

> I see human nature endowed with capabilities immeasurable of perfection; and without it, I regard and treat the whole of my race as the mere dramatis personae of a farce; of which I am myself, when performing with such fellow-actors, a principal buffoon. (140)

In a later declaration of her intense love for Albert, Elinor even anticipates Emily Brontë's Catherine Earnshaw: 'if the whole world were annihilated, and he remained . . . I should think my existence divine!' (149). The heroic phrasing suggests that Burney admired this feeling, even if her reason told her, in Harleigh's words, that the passions are not 'guides to glory,' but 'the subtlest enemies of every virtue!' (174). Elinor's romantic passion opens welcome vistas out of the conspicuously narrow, sterile world of this novel, ruled by old bachelors and widows

(Doody, *Burney* 328). The liveliest passion most of them feel is spite.

Nevertheless, however persuasively Burney let Elinor develop her opinions, they are, in the author's view, wrong. Even so, she accords them the respect of a reasoned rebuttal. She uses the conservative arguments of her period – that radical reformers do not realize the dangers of destroying functioning institutions, that they are not in touch with actual circumstance, that in discarding traditional law they give dangerous scope to impulse and self-indulgence. As Harleigh says (following Burke), 'the general laws of established society . . . may be ameliorated, changed, or reformed, by experience, wisely reflecting upon the past; by observation, keenly marking the present; or by genius, creatively anticipating the future,' but 'can never be wholly reversed, without risking a rebound that simply restores them to their original condition' (192).[38]

Elinor's enthusiasm for the French Revolution blinds her to the danger of wiping out all traditional wisdom and to the excesses of the Reign of Terror. She rejoices that it has inaugurated a 'glorious epoch, that lifts our minds from slavery and from nothingness, into play and vigour; and leaves us no longer, as heretofore, merely making believe that we are thinking beings' (10). But Burney would question the quality of this 'thinking' as proceeding more from imagination than from reason – inspiring, perhaps, but not solidly grounded in the possibilities of human life. Elinor further reveals her doctrinaire faith in abstract reason by her confidence that the truth is simple and easy to see – 'No ifs . . . I hate the whole tribe of dubiosity' (139) – and her refusal to admit that there could be anything that should not be dragged into the open. Many feminists today would agree with Burney that truth is not quite so simple and clear-cut.

Elinor is good-hearted, but, because she rejects religious principle, not reliably so. She befriends Juliet, but only after

Harleigh has taken the lead. In contrast to Harleigh and the Admiral, who help Juliet from Christian charity, Elinor is motivated partly by her doctrinaire impulse to defy convention; when Juliet refuses to display herself so as to shock upper-class propriety, Elinor is tempted to withdraw her support. It is only after Aunt Maple demands that 'the woman from France should be sent to the kitchen' that Elinor's generosity prevails over her anger and stimulates her to defend Juliet from insult: 'The spirit of contradiction, which was termed by Elinor the love of independence, fixed her design of supporting the stranger' (44, 46). When she organizes an amateur performance of *The Provoked Husband*, she casts several of the parts

> chiefly . . . for the pleasure of giving a lesson in democracy to Aunt Maple; . . . Sir Francis Wronghead to Mr Stubbs, an old steward belonging to Lord Rockton; Count Basset to young Gooch, a farmer's son; Myrtylla to Golding, her own maid, and John Moody to Tomlinson, the footman. (61–2)

Elinor has a child's delight in defying her elders, a child's inability to resist her impulses (171), and a child's thoughtlessness. In the first scene, while Harleigh is immediately moved by Juliet's desperation to help her, Elinor indulges in flippant pleasantries. She is not snobbish or malicious, like the others; but she shows no sign of humane responsibility. She is titillated by the mysterious stranger, as she was by the excitement of the French Revolution; her obliviousness to Juliet's unhappiness parallels her discounting of the sufferings produced by the Reign of Terror (9–10). When her impulses prompt, she is kind and helpful, generous with presents and with patronage; she gives herself considerable trouble to get customers for Juliet and Gabriella's little shop. But she is also capable of gloating over Juliet's approaching misery as companion to Mrs Ireton and even of sneering at the meanness of mind that would stoop to such employment, when she ought to know that this is Juliet's only means of supporting herself (454). It is Juliet, not Elinor, who feels sympathy for working people.

Unlike the Christian faith of Juliet and Harleigh, Elinor's idealism is compatible with self-centeredness. Her lofty principles do not lead her to help others. She thinks she is demonstrating her heroism by suicide, but she plans her attempts to disturb other people as much as possible, notably when she times one to coincide with Juliet's mounting the stage for the public recital that already has her in a state of anxiety. She constantly sets up scenarios involving herself, Harleigh and Juliet; her insistence on dragging Juliet into her love declarations to Harleigh, disregarding Juliet's delicacy as well as any feelings she may have for him, is blatantly selfish – and to be expected, Burney would say, in one who has cast off the restraining laws of social behavior. She is either too self-absorbed to realize the pain she is inflicting or has deluded herself that anyone who controls her feelings cannot have strong feelings to control. Characteristically, she responds to Juliet's protests: 'Fear no consequences for me! Those who know truly how to love, know how to die, as well as how to live!' (149). Elinor outrageously overdramatizes herself, in her inflated diction as well as her flamboyant threats of public suicide.

These repeated attempts demonstrate why Christians condemn suicide, for they are egotistical exploitation of others. She uses suicide as a device to gain attention and to cause other people distress and guilt. The fact that her attempts always fail suggests unconscious insincerity in her wish to die, and, to do her justice, she is honest enough to suspect this in herself. The issue of suicide was important in Burney's critique of Elinor's wholesale rejection of traditional belief, because it illustrated so definitely the divergence between religious law and individual moral speculation. Elinor insists in her debate with Harleigh that she is defending suicide on rational grounds, but Burney shows, in all her novels, that people attempt suicide because they have abandoned themselves to their emotions.[39]

Like actual radicals of the 1790s, Elinor would like to think of herself as a pure rationalist; but in fact she is controlled by her passions. These glaringly belie her feminist theory of equality and independence by making her helplessly dependent on Harleigh.[40] Ironically, and naturally in Burney's view, Elinor's freedom in indulging her passions leads her to become a slave to them – even as she insists that she is more rational than those women who conform to established rules. Although Burney was aware that these rules restricted women, she believed that they could respect themselves and exercise some control over their lives only if they used their reason to control their impulses. That is why it is Juliet, not bold Elinor, who can keep up her courage through setback after setback.

Although Elinor loudly insists on her right to proclaim her love for the man of her choice, she cannot actually do so without painful embarrassment. In the course of vainly trying 'to persuade herself', as well as Juliet, that she is 'perfectly at her ease,' she gives herself away by fleeing to generalities to avoid coming to her point: 'What amazing, unaccountable fools . . . have we all been for these quantities of centuries!' Juliet

> observed, with mingled censure and pity, the strong conflict in the mind of Elinor, between ungoverned inclination, which sought new systems for its support; and an innate feeling of what was due to the sex that she was braving, and the customs that she was scorning. (140–1)

Today the 'innate feeling' would be attributed to socialization rather than nature, but it is psychologically true: Elinor's expectation that she can simply cast off the effects of her own upbringing and society's beliefs is characteristically unrealistic.

Elinor was partly inspired by a fictitious and partly by a real-life prototype. Hays's Emma Courtney (1796), a heroine who achieved notoriety by pursuing the hero with her love, was also expert at rationalizing her emotions with feminist theorizing.

Elinor is a far more skillfully drawn version of that character, more solidly conceived and steadily viewed. Burney showed how the rejection of traditional law in favor of untried theories is related to emotional overindulgence, and made clear where her character goes wrong. Hays presented Emma as a wronged paragon, who loses her man only through unfortunate circumstance; she is also irritatingly self-righteous and lacking in humor and self-criticism. Although Hays asserted in her preface that Emma is meant to be overemotional, she did not make the point clear, and readers understandably missed it. Elinor's words are sometimes stilted, but her basic character is convincing, as well as interesting and original.

Mary Wollstonecraft provided a model for Elinor's eloquence, penetration, nobility of character and self-destructive indulgence in emotion. Elinor's rational demolition of conventional morality is closely based on arguments such as this in the *Vindication*, attacking Gregory's insistence on propriety and deference to public opinion: 'how absurd and tyrannic it is thus to lay down a system of slavery; or to attempt to educate moral beings by any other rules than those deduced from pure reason, which applies to the whole species' (117). The source for Elinor's overemotionality can be found in William Godwin's 'Memoirs' of Wollstonecraft in her *Posthumous Works* (1798). Although Godwin insisted on her purity and nobility – and Burney emphasized Elinor's chastity – his account could easily be read as a dreadful object lesson in what could happen when a woman cast off the constraints of propriety and traditional morality. Wollstonecraft's affair with Gilbert Imlay demonstrated the misery and humiliation a woman would bring on herself by pursuing a man and living with him unmarried. Imlay did not, to use the eighteenth-century term, 'esteem' her; and so he exploited and repeatedly betrayed her. Since she could not control her passion for him, she not only failed to break off their relationship, but twice attempted suicide when he abandoned her. Her intelligence did not save her from denying the obvious facts that Imlay was unworthy and their relationship hopeless.

As Wollstonecraft went to Revolutionary France to relieve her mind after her earlier love disappointment with Henry Fuseli (Godwin 100), Elinor embraced the new ideas with particular eagerness because she was fretting over the conflict between her engagement to Dennis and her love for Albert (142). Like Elinor, Wollstonecraft suffered from intense mood swings, from elation to despair, which Godwin attributed to exquisite sensibility (112). Elinor's exaggerated enthusiasm, her wild confidence in her schemes and her rapid, incoherent speech when excited are accurate symptoms of the manic state. Her mental instability helps to explain and partly excuses her chimerical ideas. Elinor's excesses, her lack of consideration and religion, and her mental instability discredit her feminism – and, Burney implies, are bound up with it.

The author's final evaluation of Elinor, at the end of the book, is ambiguous. Burney never refutes Elinor's feminist arguments, as she makes Harleigh explicitly refute her justification of suicide (Cutting, 'A Wreath for Fanny Burney's Last Novel, 60). Both Juliet and Harleigh retain their admiration and concern for her. Harleigh assures Juliet that Elinor's fine mind will eventually show her the error of trying to 'tread down the barriers of custom and experience, raised by the wisdom of foresight, and established, after trial, for public utility' (827); and, when we last see her, she seems to be doing just that, although she considers this a painful defeat. Finally, by not mentioning her in the ingenuous final reckoning of all the other significant characters, which lists the deserving ones who are invited to visit the Harleighs and the undeserving ones who are excluded, Burney pointedly avoids making a definitive judgment on Elinor. Elinor scorns the modesty and decorum which were practically as important as chastity, to say nothing of obliging compliance and respect for her elders, and flouts all the superficial standards that Burney maintained in her life and in the heroines and explicit teaching of her novels. But Burney does not pillory her as sinful, foolish or ridiculous; instead, she endows her with high qualities and sympathetically analyzes what is wrong with her position. The whole presentation is a thoughtful conservative criticism of doctrinaire radicalism, without any of the hysteria or narrow closed-mindedness found in such critics as Richard Polwhele and Hannah More.[41]

Elinor's enthusiasm for original ideas and her disdain for practical reality make her a far more convincing illustration of the dangers of imagination than Camilla or Mrs Berlinton. We can believe that she is deficient in judgment, in diffidence, and in feminine propriety because she has left her mind 'abandoned, uncontrolled, to imagination' (380). She also, of course, displays the sensibility and emotional excess that Burney linked with imagination. Since it idealized strong feelings and extreme sensitivity, sensibility could lead to suicide and condone it. By encouraging unrealistic expectations, sensibility/ imagination had opened the way for the inordinate utopian hopes of the French Revolution, which inevitably collapsed into chaos and bloodshed; for instance, in the *Example of France, a Warning to Britain*, Arthur Young traced a line from sensibility to excessive optimism to the Reign of Terror (Todd 53, 131).

The balance between Elinor and Juliet is better defined and more coherent than that between imagination/spontaneity and prudence/law in *Camilla*. Elinor's passion and original thinking set her above her stagnant society, but are discredited by her self-indulgence, extremism and impracticality. Juliet lacks her grand qualities, but excels her in the rational good sense, thoughtfulness and fortitude that Burney considered more valuable to the individual and society. Neither Elinor's theories nor Juliet's traditional wisdom can be relied on as objective truth.

Elinor's incisive attacks on respectable convention recall

those of Mrs Arlbery, but, by the time she wrote *The Wanderer*, Burney evidently felt that the oppression of women required deeper consideration than the playful barbs of an individual fortunate enough to be able to arrange her life as she liked. Elinor is committed to an ideology. It is misguided, for it brings her to personal unhappiness and is potentially dangerous to society; but it is an attempt to deal with problems that must be seriously addressed.

VI

Conclusion: Tensions Between Form and Content

LIKE MOST AUTHORS, Burney had to express her perceptions of women's situation in the form that was available and
seemed appropriate. In some ways this form was suited to her,
but it also intensified the pressure on her to conform to conventional views of woman's nature and place, and forced her
to turn to indirect means for expressing what she had to say
about certain essential issues.

Inspired by the sentimental novels of Richardson, women
developed a form in which they could express their concern
with congenial marriage, their perception of social nuances,
their values of sensitivity and consideration. Set in the home
and small social parties that were women's milieu, centering
on a young woman, these novels were organized around her
choice of marriage partner – the crucial choice for most
women, since to such a large extent it determined their life-
styles and chances for happiness and fulfillment. This was a
form in which women could use their knowledge, assert their
values and explore the issues important to them.

But the form had its limitations. While it expressed women's
concerns, it also defined them in a conventional way as personal relationships, courtship and refined feelings. The novel's
emphasis on private life – women's sphere – turned it from
social or political issues, including criticism of the social
institutions that oppressed women. Women readers were
assumed to prefer, and women writers were expected to
provide, 'the interesting and pathetic,' particularly as evoked

in a love scene (*Critical Review*, December 1782, p. 416). Since these novels relied for interest on feelings rather than events, authors unable to analyze feelings with Richardsonian depth and subtlety resorted to spinning out emotions unduly or artificially heightening them. Limiting the plot to courtship usually led to tediously drawn-out complications to prolong suspense until the final happy marriage. Ending the novel with marriage – Evelina writes, after her union with Orville, 'All is over' (406) – ruled out from fiction the largest part of women's lives. With a few exceptions, such as Lennox's *Euphemia* (1790), middle-aged women were relegated to subsidiary roles. Women's novels typically present a heroine whose problems are largely sentimental – getting rid of uncongenial suitors and clearing up misunderstandings in order to arrive at an ideal marriage; their implication is that sentimental problems are the only ones women have.

Charlotte Smith, who was unusually dissatisfied with traditional limitations, was the only woman novelist to protest explicitly against this convention. In *The Banished Man* (1794), she makes a hard-pressed woman novelist complain of the discordance between the life she lives and the life she must write about: after a painful interview with a bill collector, she must try to earn money to meet his demands by writing 'a tender dialogue' between some damsel of superlative perfection and 'her hero, who, to the bravery and talents of Caesar, adds the gentleness of Sir Charles Grandison and the wit of Lovelace'.

> But Mr. Tough's conversation, his rude threats, and his boisterous remonstrances have totally sunk her spirits; nor are they elevated by hearing that the small beer is almost out; that the pigs of a rich farmer, her next neighbour, have broke into the garden, rooted up the whole crop of peas, and not left her a single hyacinth or jonquil. (2:224–8)

In the preface to this book, Smith suggested, but did not dare to carry out, the experiment of creating a plot that did not turn on love.

Since the novel was to culminate in a happy marriage, its heroine had to be marriageable – that is, young and beautiful. She could not have the interest produced by experience and a fully formed character, and her beauty tended to reduce her to a sexual object. Women authors tried to deal with this problem by insisting on the primary importance of intellectual and moral qualities, but still yielded to the convention of beautiful heroines. Tompkins's extensive reading of novels of the period turned up only one example of a plain heroine (*The Popular Novel in England 1770–1800* 150–1). In real life, Burney resented men's overemphasis on women's appearance;[42] in her fiction, she compromised with the convention. Evelina and Juliet are so beautiful that they attract every eye. She thought of making Cecilia 'unbeautiful' (*DL* 1:344), although in the end she did not dare to do so. Camilla is insistently described as lovely, but she is conspicuously less beautiful than her cousin, Indiana, whose empty head and selfish character are savagely emphasized. Burney reinforces her point by satirizing the fatuity of the otherwise intelligent Melmond, who persists in believing that Indiana's outward beauty indicates inward beauty and in seeing her silliness as charming femininity.

The heroine was further limited by her need to be an exemplar. Eighteenth-century readers expected to find edifying models in fiction. Anna Barbauld mentioned in defense of novels that a work like *Cecilia* provided 'ideas of delicacy and refinement' that many young women could not gain from any society they had access to (*British Novelists* 1:48). Miss Coussmaker, a friend of the Burney family, remarked admiringly, 'Not any one character in La Nouvelle Heloise gave me half the Idea of nobleness, generosity, & goodness' that *Evelina* had (qtd Hemlow 90).

Unfortunately, it was not the qualities Miss Coussmaker

listed that were in fact considered essential in women, and therefore to be emphasized in exemplars. Rather, it was Barbauld's 'delicacy and refinement,' together with prudence, modesty, self-control and propriety. 'Propriety,' wrote Hannah More, is 'the first, the second, the third requisite' for female virtue.

> A woman may be knowing, active, witty, and amusing; but without propriety she cannot be amiable. . . . It shows itself by a regular, orderly, undeviating course; and never starts from its sober orbit into any splendid eccentricities; for it would be ashamed of such praise as it might extort by any aberrations from its proper path. It renounces all commendation but what is characteristic. (1:6–7)

Thus extraordinary accomplishments of any kind would jeopardize the 'amiability' on which women depended for their self-esteem as well as the security of their social position, and would occasion shame rather than pride because they would not be 'characteristic': that is, appropriate to a narrowly defined female role. Conformity becomes a virtue.

A fictional heroine was expected to live up to even higher standards than those required of actual women, and, because of the negative nature of these standards, she could hardly avoid being colorless. To be above blame, a character had to be totally chaste, dutiful, decorous and refined. In real life, Elizabeth Griffith could admit to the man she loved that her chastity was not impregnable, forgive him for propositioning her, accept him when he proposed, marry him under conditions of humiliating secrecy and live with him happily ever after; fictional heroines, including her own, could make no such compromises. It may be that Mrs Tyrold's perfectionist excesses, which contrast with Burney's own behavior as a wife and mother, were intended to make her an exemplar rather than the rigid extremist she appears to modern readers. Even male writers such as Henry Fielding kept their heroines more innocent than their heroes, but this was more incumbent on women writers, who were subject to narrower moral standards.[43] Respectable ladies had won the right to be professional writers, but they had to be punctiliously careful about the moral tendency of their works. They were expected to enforce orthodox morality; it was assumed that a virtuous female would not think of challenging conventional codes or authority.

Charlotte Smith, the only woman to complain explicitly of the obligatory limitations on her heroines, explained the reasons for their flatness. First, 'very young women [Althea, the heroine in question is sixteen] have no striking traits of character to distinguish them, till some circumstance in their lives either calls forth their understanding, or decides that they have none.' Secondly, 'any very marked feature' is considered to disfigure a heroine. 'Too much reason and self-command destroy the interest we take in her distresses. It has even been observed, that Clarissa is so equal to every trial as to diminish our pity.' So the novelist is not free to give a heroine 'other virtues than gentleness, pity, filial obedience, or faithful attachment' (*Marchmont* [1796] 1:177–8).

Smith tried to make Althea forceful and interesting, and tells us that her unusual misfortunes produced 'that fortitude and strength of mind which gave energy to an understanding, naturally of the first class' (1:179). But she failed to demonstrate unusual energy or intelligence in Althea or any of her other heroines in the action of her books. She let Althea go to meet the hero alone when there was a compelling reason, but found it necessary to assure her readers that in most situations Althea showed 'that timid deference to the opinion of the world, which is an amiable feature in the character of a young woman' (2:150).

Burney and her contemporaries had to deal with the contradiction between the restrictive, negative ideal of femininity they were supposed to promote and their own life-style; for, by the act of writing and publishing, they violated the precepts of dependency, self-effacement and artlessness. Only an ultra-conservative like Hannah More could accept the conservative ideal outright: her Lucilla Stanley, a paragon of correctness, contributes to the stupefying dullness of *Coelebs in Search of a Wife* (1809). Most women wanted to promote a female ideal who illustrated some of their own positive qualities, as well as to center their novels on an interesting character. They generally compromised by explicitly endowing their heroine with strength and intelligence, but not allowing her to display them in action, and all the while insisting upon her softness and propriety. The characters are made inconsistent by their authors' conflicting allegiance to independent thinking and 'reasonable' conformity, self-reliance and sweet dependency, mature understanding and innocent simplicity.

Burney shared the general wish to endow her heroines with intelligence and strength, but seems also to have been genuinely attracted to the simplicity that was part of the conventional ideal. She may have been expressing nostalgia for the relative freedom of childhood (Spacks, 'Ev'ry Woman' 45), and she may have associated simplicity with spontaneity, although the eighteenth-century idea of female simplicity was more socialized than natural. Burney presented Evelina as 'the offspring of Nature, and of Nature in her simplest attire' (B), despite the fact that her attractively modest manners, her evaluation of good and ill breeding and her correct attitudes on feminine behavior have to be the product of careful training. Camilla is simultaneously exhorted to dissimulate the many feelings that her parents consider discreditable and praised for artlessness of the most extreme kind. Edgar is moved to rhapsody by her 'clear transparent singleness of mind, so beautiful in its total ignorance of every species of scheme, every sort of double measure, every idea of secret view and latent expedient!' (671) The curious overestimation of Eugenia by every virtuous character in the book results presumably from her perfect freedom from guile (373).

Conclusion: tensions between form and content

Since the theme of *Cecilia* requires a rational protagonist and that of *The Wanderer* a resolute one, simplicity is idealized only in secondary female characters of those novels. Henrietta Belfield is insistently described as innocent and artless, and, at one point, Cecilia even seems to feel Henrietta is superior to her in (feminine) goodness (441). Although there is no question of Cecilia's superiority, Henrietta's naïveté, humble unpretentiousness and gushing emotions are supposed to be admirable as well as endearing; and Mrs Thrale loved her (*DL* 2:139).

The Wanderer offers the most striking example of Burney's divided allegiance between the ideals of human adequacy for women and artless innocence. The much-tried Juliet could not survive if she were simple, but she is paired with her half-sister Lady Aurora, who has nothing to do in the novel but be sweet. Contemplating the sleeping Aurora before taking what she thinks is a final farewell, Juliet sees her as an angel.

> The touching innocence of her countenance; the sweetness which no sadness could destroy; the grief exempt from impatience; and the air of purity that overspread her whole face, and seemed breathing round her whole form, inspired Juliet . . . with ideas too sublime for mere sublunary sorrow. She knelt, with tender reverence, by her side, . . . Then, placing gently upon her bosom the written farewell, she softly kissed the hem of her garments, and glided from the room. (811–12)

Since Juliet is herself as virtuous as anyone could possibly be, her veneration seems to indicate that she has been contaminated by experience itself. This is confirmed by Gregory, who wrote that 'Virgin purity is of that delicate nature, that it cannot hear certain things without contamination' (35). If purity is an essential part of female virtue, and if it is so fragile that it cannot withstand the stress of growing up (even Lady Aurora will be corrupted by experience some day), women are inevitably trapped in moral inadequacy if not guilt. Burney's presentation of Aurora and Camilla shows that she could not wholly resist the appeal of a reductive simplicity, based on ignorance and incompatible with maturity.

But of course it is Juliet who is the center of interest, and Burney does her best to show her mental and moral strength, while protecting her femininity. Juliet is mentally independent, confident of her own judgment regardless of what other people say. She shares her creator's capacity to become interested and learn in any situation not totally depressing – as when she observes and appreciates life on the farm to which she has fled from her husband's pursuit (663, 665). She can calmly repel Lord Melbury's proposition and excuse the culprit because of his youth and inexperience. However, her intelligence is shown passively by correct judgment; it is Harleigh who argues against Elinor's erroneous opinions. And Juliet never deviates from conventional morality. Despite the facts that her husband is odious, that he cares only for her money, that her marriage was coerced and probably invalid, she can hardly restrain herself from following him back to France, driven 'by an overwhelming dread that to resist might possibly be wrong' (810).

The self-reliant resolution that Juliet repeatedly demonstrates throughout the novel would be remarkable even today. Burney attributed spirit and courage to all her heroines and contrived situations in which they could display them in an impeccably feminine manner. But her earlier effects are not convincing. Burney makes an opportunity for Evelina to prevent Macartney from committing suicide, while preserving her delicacy by alternating decisive acts with helpless tremblings and faintings. Cecilia is given a similar opportunity when Harrel commits suicide, inspiring young Delvile to rhapsodize over her sensible (but not remarkably heroic) conduct: 'such spirit with such softness! so much presence of mind with such feeling!' (422). Camilla refrains from fleeing before a friendly bull.

Burney could demonstrate Juliet's courage more convincingly because she departed from the genteel conventions of ladies' fiction by artificially declassing her. Juliet, faced with the unladylike need to support herself, manages to maintain her spirits in spite of painfully lowered expectations: the 'hope of self-dependence, ever cheering to an upright mind', 'sweetened' her rest 'in her mean little apartment, though with no brighter prospect than that of procuring a laborious support,' by working for a milliner (205). As a temporary member of the working class, Juliet finds herself walking alone in the country and is threatened with rape by two louts. Her resourcefulness in frightening and distracting them from their purpose is impressive even in twentieth-century terms. Juliet demonstrates, as Burney herself did, a courage that is both genuine and feminine: 'the effect of secret reasoning, and cool calculation of consequences, [more] than of fearless temperament, or inborn bravery' (213).[44]

Nevertheless, Burney felt it necessary to reassure her readers about her heroine's true femininity. It is delicacy that is 'the prominent feature of her character' (818). In one of the very passages where she is praising Juliet's resolution, Burney takes care to point out that nothing short of destitution could have stimulated her to try to make money (197). The same letter from her mentor that urges Juliet to exertion and declares that human beings of either sex must learn to be self-sufficient specifies 'female exertion' and assumes it is necessary for women to combat inherent bodily weakness and timidity (204).

Burney's preoccupation with self-reliance goes back to one of her earliest works, *The Witlings*. Her most explicit statement on the subject appears in the concluding speech of that play – where it stands out strikingly because it does not fit its situation. Beaufort says to Cecilia:

> . . . let us . . . hope that our Example . . . may inculcate this most useful of all practical precepts: That self-dependance is the first of Earthly Blessings; since those who rely solely on others for support & protection are not only liable to the common

vicissitudes of Human Life, but exposed to the partial caprices
& infirmities of Human Nature.

This invigorating moral comes as a surprise, because dependence is only a subordinate element in the plot. (Beaufort is
financially dependent upon Lady Smatter, who forbade him to
marry Cecilia when the banker who had charge of her fortune
went bankrupt.) The lovers become independent only in the
sense that they now have money to live on, which they
acquired not through their own initiative, but through Cen-
sor's threat to torment Lady Smatter with lampoons if she does
not approve the marriage, together with his gift to Cecilia of a
five-thousand-pound portion.

Although Burney's three later novels demonstrate the
misery of dependence in great detail, she never again spelled
out the human need for independence. Even Juliet no longer
seeks and values self-dependence when she has her family
and Harleigh. If women ceased to rely 'on others for support &
protection,' what would happen to the patriarchal family?[45]
Significantly, when Burney wrote of her father's difficulties in
marrying while he was still an apprentice, she specified 'the
high *male* value of self-dependence' (*Memoirs* 1:69–70; my
italics).

Smith's reference to Clarissa in her analysis of the acceptable
heroine indicates the importance of pathetic appeal. As Brissenden has brilliantly demonstrated, the most exquisite sentimental appeal was generated by the sufferings of a blameless
victim: the spectacle of virtue in distress. Few late eighteenth-
century novelists could resist it. The distresses of the heroine
did represent those of real women – disregard of their feelings,
for example, in a world ordered by male priorities and self-
interest. But too often both the distresses and the rhetoric that
expresses them are so exaggerated that they become ends in
themselves rather than illustrations of genuine, actual problems. Sympathetic readers would derive purely emotional

pleasure from weeping with a character they loved; unsympathetic ones would dismiss her problems as factitious.

Emotional indulgence that began and ended with sympathetic tears did not threaten the established order. The pleasure depended on the fact that no disturbing questions were being raised; the heroine's personal problems could be solved with personal good feeling, without any changes except in the hearts of some erring characters. Since it did not prompt to action or open up any alternative to conventional thinking, this kind of emotionality had none of the subversive possibilities of the warmth, impulsiveness and free imagination already described in Chapters Five and Six. The more properly the heroine conducted herself, the more satisfyingly pathetic she was. In this way, the emotionality that might seem to be a release from legalistic morality actually had the effect of reinforcing it. Weeping over distressed virtue was supposed to be of intrinsic moral value, as it demonstrated one's tender heart and appreciation of virtue. It thus fitted into the general aim of edifying the reader and was appropriately complemented by direct moralizing.

Contemporary criticism of Burney's novels reflects these expectations of women's fiction. Miss Coussmaker was delightfully distressed by the 'tragical' reunion of father and daughter in *Evelina*, which 'worked' her 'as much as the death of Desdemona or Belvidera'; she also declared that Villars's letters 'would have done honour even to the pen of a Johnson' (qtd Hemlow 90–1). Burke praised *Cecilia* for 'the natural vein of humour, the tender pathetic, [and] the comprehensive and noble moral' (*DL* 2:92–4). The following appreciation of *Cecilia* by three highly-placed, intellectual women illustrates the gap between eighteenth-century and present-day expectations of fiction and its effects on evaluation:

> 'If you speak . . . of the morality of the book,' cried the Duchess [of Portland], with a solemn sort of voice, 'we shall, indeed,

> never give Miss Burney her due: so striking, so pure, so gen-
> uine, so instructive.' 'Yes,' cried Mrs. Chapone, 'let us com-
> plain how we will of the torture she has given our nerves, we
> must all join in saying she has bettered us by every line.' 'No
> book,' said Mrs. Delany, 'ever was so useful as this, because
> none other that is so good was ever so much read.' (*DL* 2:201)

Dr Burney found the 'moral tendencies' of *Camilla* 'so numer-
ous, delicate and free from severity and cant, that the work
seems to me the best and most impressive system of female
education that I have ever seen' (*Fanny Burney and the Burneys*
223). A reviewer in the *Monthly Review* recommended the book
'as a guide for the conduct of young females in the most important circumstances . . . of life' and compared Mr Tyrold's letter
to a large and lustrous diamond (October 1796, p. 163). It was
only natural that Frances Burney would acquiesce in this
praise and respond to it by accentuating the pathos and
moralizing that were so enthusiastically approved.

Women's novels were limited by the expectations that they
would deal with personal relations centering on a courtship
situation; that their central character would be a young,
innocent and well-conducted young lady; that they would be
adorned with pathetic scenes and fortified with unexception-
able moral instruction. Working within these conventions
made it difficult to deal with many subjects, including problems that were not sentimental in origin and criticism of
established authority. The writers had to express their concerns indirectly, by resorting to contrived twists of plot or
investing events with more intense emotion than was appropriate. Instead of representing the ordinary problems and
misjudgments that women had to deal with, authors spun out
unlikely misunderstandings and jealousies to delay the marriage that had to complete the action. Secret marriages recur in
novel after novel and generate enormous guilt and anxiety.
Rejected with indignation or followed by remorse, the secret
marriage appears to be a substitute for the seduction that could

not be permitted a heroine destined for a happy ending. It was a way of associating sexual guilt with a heroine who had to preserve her chastity, and, like seduction, it entailed a man's exploiting and devaluing a woman in order to gratify his vanity or lust. Cecilia's shame and outrage at Delvile's proposal of a secret marriage would be appropriate if he had tried to seduce her.

A fault-free protagonist could not incur misfortunes or even adventures by her own initiative. Her problems had to be precipitated by contrived unlucky circumstances. Plot developments in these novels seem gratuitous and unconvincing because they do not develop from character – hence the dissociation between plot and character that Tompkins has identified as the endemic flaw in the later eighteenth-century novel (*The Popular Novel* 346–7). To sustain their readers' emotional involvement despite this implausibility, authors exaggerated the intensity of their plot complications, as well as the rhetoric in which they dramatized them.

These novels produce recurrent dissatisfaction because of the discrepancy between the situations presented and the emotions called for. This point can be clarified by reference to the first part of *A Simple Story*. Inchbald had no hidden agenda: her subject genuinely was psychological obstacles on the way to a marriage between two people who love each other. She could develop her theme with interest and plausibility because she was willing to show faults in both the heroine and the eminently virtuous hero. Because she is passionate and self-willed and he is rigid, they engage in conflict and are responsible for what happens to them. Inchbald did not have to resort to the usual unfounded jealousies and unnecessary misunderstandings. The situation is believable because the characters are, and therefore it generates its own emotional force even though feelings are expressed in the plainest diction. Because her fable directly and sufficiently expresses her meaning, Inchbald does not need to supply feeling and significance by inflating her rhetoric.

Frances Burney: the World of 'Female Difficulties'

Novelists who built on the traditions established by Burney and her contemporaries were able to develop similar themes with less stringent inhibitions. Austen, writing in the same convention, transcended it by letting her heroines have enough minor faults to make them realistically interesting; but this required confidence developed over several generations. Delvile's pride of family when he explains why he could not give up his name to marry Cecilia (501–4) offends her as Darcy's offends Elizabeth Bennet in his first, rejected proposal – but in *Pride and Prejudice* (1813) the situation is more plausible, for Darcy objects to Elizabeth's unpresentable relatives, a more common obstacle than a freak clause in a will. Darcy's arrogance and Elizabeth's vulgar connections would have disqualified them as eighteenth-century sentimental lovers. Burney wanted to embarrass Evelina by placing her in a situation similar to Elizabeth's, but giving her an ill-bred, obtuse mother and sisters would have been seen as contaminating the heroine's own gentility. Hence Evelina must be practically dissociated from her own grandmother and cousins by the unlikely devices of two disproportionate marriages, one of them disputed, and adoption by her grandfather's tutor.

Burney's own life supplied her with more genuine challenges than she allowed her heroines; she met them with more convincing courage and described them with more moving, because more authentic, language. Her journals show her developing from a sharply observant but timid girl, shrinking from self-assertion and fearful of deviating from propriety, into a mature woman of impressive strength and resolution, one who could get what was important to her and deal with situations that would test a liberated contemporary woman. At the age of fifty-nine, she sustained a breast amputation alone because she knew her husband could not bear to watch it; at sixty-three, she traveled alone through wartime Germany without money, passport, or knowledge of the language; at sixty-five, she spent a night clinging to a rock because, in her enthusiasm for collecting mineral specimens, she had not noticed the tide coming in. (Characteristically, she was moved to comment: 'What a situation for a Female Alone' [*JL* 10:701.])

She rendered these fearful crises in plain language, letting the facts speak for themselves. She described her mastectomy with clinical detail and accuracy, and totally without feminine trepidations, factitious working-up of her pain and fear, sentimental excess of any kind – or the least flourish of her own courage. How this restrained account of actual suffering contrasts with the effusive falsity of her descriptions of sentimental suffering in her fictional heroines! Although Burney tried to shape herself to the same restrictive ideal as her heroines, real life presented her with challenges which she then found the resolution and independence to meet. Her heroines show the destructive effects of cultural stereotyping; she herself shows the triumph of natural character over stereotype.

Evelina is Burney's most integrated fiction because what she had to say fits nicely into the conventions of the lady's novel. Her subject is a normal seventeen-year-old's concerns and perception of the world. Evelina can be essentially faultless and still make mistakes because she is young: she can get away with a little imprudence while remaining a model because mistakes that would not be condoned in a mature woman are permissible in an inexperienced girl. She has scope to mature perceptibly, from the floundering girl who tells a foolish lie and is helplessly manipulated by Sir Clement in their first conversation to the self-possessed young woman who can put him in his place at the end of the book. Moreover, since she exists in the normal world of a sheltered seventeen-year-old, her problems consist of being ignored in a social group or getting rid of a persistent dance partner, and her mistakes do not have serious consequences. Because serious issues are not raised, the idyllic romantic ending does not provoke questions. Discordant, violent and emotionally overwrought elements can easily be ignored because they are extraneous to the main theme.

Burney had difficulties with the feminine novel, however, when she wanted to raise more significant issues and express a deeper vision. She grew increasingly impatient with its limitations, insisting that neither *Camilla* nor *The Wanderer* were mere 'love-tales' (Hemlow 339). Yet she stayed with the form, which suited her in some respects, and tried to fit what she had to say into its conventions. In *Cecilia* she bent a romantic plot to show the limitations of romantic love and marriage. The central point of interest is not whether Cecilia will marry her true love – the romantic issue – but whether she will control her own life, an issue symbolized by her keeping her name and her money. Cecilia's long-drawn hesitancies are typical of eighteenth-century sentimental courtship and could easily be attributed to the modesty considered proper to refined young women rather than to reluctance to give up her autonomy. Delvile's unwarranted suspicions about Cecilia and Belfield exemplify the complications that often kept lovers apart in those novels, and are unlikely and irrelevant in this situation. Because so much of the novel is devoted to overcoming the obstacles to Cecilia's marriage, we wonder why her happiness is pointedly circumscribed after that has been achieved. The conventional plot devices that Burney uses to express Cecilia's ambivalence and frustration – secret marriage, delirium and near approach to death – distract from her significant message because of their easy pathetic appeal. As in Camilla's crisis, the emotion is so excessive in terms of its cause that we are tempted to reject it altogether and thus lose sight of the real, though less catastrophic, pain of the heroines.

In *Camilla*, problems arose from the generic expectations that a woman's novel would present a heroine with no significant faults, culminate in a happy marriage, and preach conventional morality. Camilla cannot convincingly learn from bitter experience to correct the defects of her character if these defects are inconsequential to begin with. Burney's penetrating anatomy of Edgar's relationship with Camilla

182

belies the possibility of a happy marriage. The narrator's explicit statements affirm orthodox moral views that are undercut by evidence offered in the narrative itself: the conflict between teller and tale obscures and weakens her message.

Burney's subject in *The Wanderer* is the oppression and enforced helplessness of women, particularly in the economic area, and the adequacy or inadequacy of radical feminist solutions to these problems. But, since she was writing in the tradition of the sentimental novel, she gave protracted emphasis to contrived emotional distresses, such as those caused by Juliet's unnecessary abstention from telling Harleigh she is married. Read as the story of Juliet's outraged feelings – her agonies over whether or not to play the harp at a public concert, her embarrassment when unnecessarily dragged in to witness Elinor's love declarations to Harleigh – *The Wanderer* seems inflated and even silly. Read as an anatomy of women's difficulties in a patriarchal society, it is realistic and appropriately bleak. But readers might well miss the indictment of society because Burney invited them to expect a sentimental novel. She so insisted on Juliet's delicacy that it is hard to remember her resolution. The very phrase 'female difficulties' seems to imply that the difficulties are inherent in woman's delicate nature rather than produced by the attitudes and institutions of her society. When Juliet is constantly accosted by men as she walks alone in the country, she thinks, not that men are brutish, but that 'this hazardous plan of lonely wandering' is 'little fitted to the female character, to female safety, and female propriety' (642). The final summary of Juliet's difficulties – actual or potential assaults on her honor, offenses to her delicacy, exhaustion of her strength and calumny of her virtue (836) – stresses delicate distresses more than real problems.

This mismatch between content and form has invited misreading of *The Wanderer* as a conventional lachrymose tale of female debility. The reviewer (probably William Hazlitt) in the *Edinburgh Review*, accordingly, dismissed the book as a prolonged and exaggerated lament over 'Female Difficulties': that is 'difficulties created out of nothing' (April 1815, pp. 336–8). Joyce Hemlow emphasizes, rather, the superficial moral teaching to be expected in a sentimental novel: its 'first purpose' is 'to distinguish between propriety and impropriety, between good and faulty behaviour; to delineate and reward perfect conduct, and to describe and punish its reverse' (342). In both cases, generic expectations encouraged by Burney cause a misreading that drains the novel of lasting significance. As Juliet's resolution and competence are obscured by the delicacy required in a heroine, Elinor's originality and satiric penetration are unduly subordinated to her flamboyantly emotional role in the romance plot: her clamorous pursuit of Harleigh and her stagy suicide attempts make her appear more a slave of passion than the ardent but intelligent social critic that she was intended to be.

The conventions of the form in which Burney was writing reinforced her personal inhibitions against expressing anger at traditionally sanctioned opinion and duly constituted authority. Yet, as she became more aware of women's oppression, she felt more urgency to express it. The result was that her repressed emotions burst out uncontrollably in the form of inappropriate violence. Recent critics, notably Epstein and Doody, have argued eloquently that this violence is an effective expressive technique; but I cannot agree. I believe that Burney's gifts were for comedy and domestic realism and that she aimed to be a realistic writer.

At sixteen, she wrote in her diary: 'I cannot be much pleased without an appearance of truth; at least of possibility – I wish the story to be natural tho' the sentiments are refined; and the characters to be probable tho' their behaviour is excelling' (*ED* 1:9). She announced in the Preface to *Evelina* that she was not offering 'Romance, where Fiction is coloured by all the gay tints of luxurious Imagination, where Reason is an outcast, and where the sublimity of the *Marvellous* rejects all aid from sober Probability' (8). When readers of *Cecilia* questioned the probability of the Delviles' refusal to let Mortimer give up his family name, she vigorously argued that this was in character and cited a real-life example to substantiate her claim.[46] It was in the interests of realism that she deliberately departed from generic convention and gave her novel a mixed ending in place of the blissful marriage or tear-drenched death that her readers expected. Her intense reaction to the resulting criticism shows how important this ending was to her. She insisted, to Crisp and others, on the importance of depriving Cecilia of her fortune at the end:

> I shall think I have rather written a farce than a serious history, if the whole is to end, like the hack Italian operas, with a jolly chorus that makes all parties good and all parties happy! . . . the hero and heroine are neither plunged in the depths of misery, nor exalted to UN*human* happiness. Is not such a middle state more natural, more according to real life, and less resembling every other book of fiction? (*DL* 2:80–1)

Her defense of the novel in her Dedication to *The Wanderer* argues its moral usefulness on the assumption that it is a realistic picture of life:

> What is the species of writing that offers fairer opportunities for conveying useful precepts? It is, or it ought to be, a picture of supposed, but natural and probable human existence . . . therefore . . . it . . . gives to juvenile credulity knowledge of the world, without ruin, or repentance; and the lessons of experience, without its tears. (xx)

She goes on to disclaim any intention of writing 'a merely romantic love-tale, or a story of improbable wonders' (xxii). Burney thought of herself as a realistic writer, making her points through lifelike characters in situations that could be found in daily life. When she diverged from realism, it was because she was following generic conventions that seemed natural because they were conventions (Juliet's inability to tell Harleigh that she is married) or reaching for exalted or heart-rending effects.

Burney's principal subject was the difficulties of everyday life in society – not knowing what to say, not being able to get people to take one seriously, feeling guilty for giving a misleading impression, worrying about money. She could and did develop such themes realistically: she worked out Camilla's feelings of inadequacy and Juliet's struggles to rise above her circumstances with inventiveness and probability. She did not have to resort to far-fetched symbols like sudden madness to express predicaments, for she could find them in the circumstances of ordinary life – the ballroom where women must sit waiting to be chosen or rejected, the fact that giving up one's name at marriage is routinely expected of women but considered degrading for a man.

Much of Burney's meaning could be expressed in the comic mode. It was not necessary to drive Cecilia mad to show that people did not pay attention to her wishes: her frustration is conveyed as vigorously and more plausibly in the scenes where half her acquaintance collaborate to retard her urgent trip to London or her guardians wrangle with each other instead of settling her affairs. Burney's memorable characters are all comic ones – butts, wits, or often an artful combination of the two. Giles Arbe is a greatly improved version of the unworldly moralist first sketched in Mr Albany. Instead of reaching for grandeur, Burney fully developed Arbe's comic side, an obliviousness to common reactions that keeps him perpetually annoying or embarrassing people despite his benign intentions. Arbe's oddity gives him a genuinely original vision, so that he can see through and innocently expose shoddiness that generally passes successfully in the world, the manipulations of his showy cousin Miss Arbe or the rationalizations of rich people who exploit those who work for their living. Elinor Joddrel succeeds as a character not only on account of her witty attacks on conventional thinking, but because of her ability to laugh at her own vanity and at her ostentatious but always failing suicide attempts. She is less effective when she is supposed to be sublime or tragic.

Doody has demolished the traditional view of Burney as a 'cheerful little Augustan chatterbox' (*Burney* 387). Burney concerned herself with serious issues, questioned established authority, expressed a devastating view of human deficiencies of mind and heart. *Cecilia* displays a high society of heartless fools, *Camilla* dramatizes the sufferings of an amiable girl surrounded by self-righteous authorities, *The Wanderer* exposes the platitude that good conduct and earnest effort will bring rewards. But all these points could be made through comic realism. Comedy can be grim. There was no need to resort to pathos, sublimity, melodrama or violent farce; and, unlike Dickens (to whom Doody compares her), Burney could not handle them. Her attempts at sublime effects, as in some of Albany's and Elinor's speeches, are unnatural and expressed in dreadfully stilted language. Her overstrained pathetic is false and distracts attention from realistic problems that deserve sympathy and call for redress. Her grotesque effects – the beating of Madame Duval; Juliet's fearful night in the poacher's cottage, where she sees bloodstains on the floor and fears murder – are out of place and fail to enhance the meaning or impact of the essential situation being presented. Burney's nightmare effects do not work because her surface is realistic.

I believe that a stronger case can be made for Burney's mature novels by borrowing Jane Tompkins's argument that women's novels ought not to be judged by esthetic standards that have been developed on the basis of men's novels, such as shapeliness of form, but rather by the effectiveness with which they 'work out problems inherent in the culture at the moment of composition' (qtd Kolodny 304). This is Burney's great strength. Her major themes – frustration, enforced passivity, pervasive guilt, subtle internalized constraints – resist orderly formulation.

The tension in Burney between intelligence and strength, on the one hand, and timid conformity, on the other, sensitized her to the problems of women in a society that tried to force them into passivity. She had a keen sense of the ridiculous, a free-ranging imagination and an independent mind capable of criticizing convention – yet she responded to the pressure to model herself according to a feminine ideal that prescribed modest acceptance of authority and control of disorderly impulses. This conflict led to strain and ambivalence in her novels. But it also intensified her rendition of the feelings of a woman suffering from repression. Powerlessness was of course a common theme in eighteenth-century women's novels, since it was so prominent a feature in their lives. Aggressive courtship by unwanted suitors, arbitrary dictation by parents and guardians, frustration of attempts to determine the course of their own lives were common problems for women's heroines. But more vividly than any of her contemporaries, Burney expressed the feelings of these trammeled women and analyzed the internal as well as the external restraints upon them.

What is most notable is her expression of the internalized constraints upon women, even though she could not be fully aware of them herself. If she could not openly indict virtuous parental authority, she could expose its blighting effects on Camilla. If she did not challenge the accepted doctrine of separate spheres and a sexual character, she showed how they undermined a naturally strong woman's efforts to be self-dependent. If she did not inquire why women felt chronically guilty, she drew attention to and vividly dramatized that guilt. Burney illuminated 'female difficulties' of her own time, and many of them still persist. Alison Lurie's Erica Tate is restricted by her constant need to do the right thing, as defined by the feminine mystique; Fay Weldon's Natalie Harris finds that her identity depends on her husband's position and continued favor (*The War between the Tates*, 1974; *The Heart of the Country*, 1988). The situations in which Burney dramatized such feelings may be contrived and her explicit judgments controlled by patriarchal ideology, but her expression of female impotence, embarrassment, anxiety and restriction is authentic.

Notes

1. Patricia Spacks first called attention to this revealing remark, as well as Burney's statement to the Reverend Charles de Guiffar-dière ('Mr Turbulent') that she saved herself from misbehavior by running from any risk she perceived (*Imagining a Self* 160). Spacks argues, acutely and persuasively, that Burney's journals and novels are unified by 'female fear – not of the absence of power [like *Tristram Shandy*] but of failure of goodness and consequent loss of love' (158).

2. Kristina Straub, in *Divided Fictions: Fanny Burney and Feminine Strategy* (Lexington: University Press of Kentucky, 1987), argues that the inconsistencies in Burney's novels are purposeful ren-ditions of the conflicts in her culture and her own consciousness: 'The ability to sustain and express contradiction is both a response to ideological conflicts in the culture and a strategy for female psychic survival in mid-eighteenth-century life' (3). I cannot fol-low her in finding positive value in the fact that a text contradicts itself: '*Evelina* shows us Burney's personal division . . . not as weakness or lack of artistic control, but as gaps in the ideological *bricolage* of Burney's text . . . barely articulated, incompletely formulated ideological possibilities that the text cannot, at that moment in history, fully sustain' (25).

3. Cecilia, the independent heiress, can be more decided about her preferences than Burney dared to be, resolving not to associate with mediocre people who have nothing to offer her or pursuing without concealment 'the exhaustless fund of entertainment which reading, that richest, highest, and noblest source of intel-lectual enjoyment, perpetually affords' (31). While Burney's guiding principle was to avoid doing wrong, Cecilia's was 'to ACT RIGHT' (55). D. D. Devlin discusses ways in which the fiction of the novels allowed her to attack established views and

institutions as she could not in the direct form of the journals, such as developing characters whom, in real life or in life as reported in her journals, she would have had to condemn and dismiss: 'she could in her fiction stay with them a little and allow her imagination to admit other possible ways in which women might confront their destiny' (93).

4. Cf. Juliet, who, though normally gentle, finds courage when her hostess, Mrs Howel, discovers that she is a dependent and treats her with 'haughty distance'; 'for courage, where there is any nobleness of mind, always rises highest, when oppressive pride seeks to crush it by studied humiliation' (119).

5. See, for instance, letters to Lady Bute of 6 March 1753 and 10 October 1753. It must be noted, however, that in old age Burney rigorously edited all her papers, removing, for example, hostile references to her stepmother (Hemlow 35).

6. For example, she noted with relief, 'I have now a little broke my father into sending excuses' (*DL* 2:253).

7. Two works that do convincingly represent a young woman's point of view are Elizabeth Griffith's *A Series of Genuine Letters between Henry and Frances* (1757–70), a slightly fictionalized version of the Griffiths' actual love-letters during courtship and marriage, which Burney read at sixteen and 'prodigiously' liked (*ED* 1:9), and Frances Brooke's *The History of Emily Montague* (1769), an epistolary novel on the same theme. In both books, young women directly express their thoughts and feelings about everyday experience, although they are not so convincingly adolescent as Evelina. But neither book is enlivened by Burney's humor and social satire. They are thoroughgoing sentimental novels, mostly confined to the feelings and opinions of young people in a courtship situation. The Griffiths' opinions on female nature and behavior would have appealed to Burney: they both believed that women had intelligence that should be cultivated; Henry was constantly educating Frances, who called him her 'guide, guardian, kinsman, father, friend'; she felt 'insurmountable Bashfulness' about being 'a female Author'; Henry praised Frances for valuing her excellence as a woman above her excellence as an author (2:102; 4:171, 254).

8. Burney's lasting sensitivity to male encroachment is brought out by an incident to which Patricia Spacks has drawn attention. During her years at Court, she was frequently troubled by 'Mr. Turbulent,' a fellow attendant on the Queen. He was a well-

meaning but intrusive man who constantly assaulted Burney's
reserve by advocating shocking views, making intimate confidences, paying her extravagantly gallant compliments – doing
anything to force a response from her. She could not control him
or avoid him; all she could do was assume an icy reserve – which,
of course, restricted her more than him and had the further effect
of depriving her of the only lively companionship available to her
at the time (*DL* 3:235). On one occasion, he provoked her into
plainly expressing her feeling of entrapment and consequent
resentment. 'What choice has a poor female,' she asked, 'with
whom she may converse? Must she not, in company as in dancing, take up with those who choose to take up with her?' She
went on to retaliate in the only way open to her, by denying him
the gratification of thinking that her compliance was voluntary:
'No man . . . has any cause to be flattered that a woman talks
with him, while it is only in reply; for though *he* may come, go,
address or neglect, and do as he will – she, let her think and wish
what she may, must only follow as he leads' (*DL* 3:215; Spacks,
Imagining a Self 169).

9. Straub eloquently develops the miserable situation of Mrs
   Mirvan, especially on pp. 26, 57–60.
10. Straub points out that the backers' concern for their protégées in
    the race between old women staged by the dissolute aristocrats is
    the ultimate travesty of the gallantry practiced toward ladies (45–
    6).
11. Despite an emphasis on ill breeding that verges on snobbery,
    Burney had a definite respect for middle-class businessmen. Mr
    Tedman, a rich grocer, is one of the more decent people in *The
    Wanderer*. Cf. Henrietta Belfield's delicate criticism of her high-
    minded brother: 'I think . . . that it is a great disgrace to my poor
    father's honest memory, to have us turn beggars after his death,
    when he left us all so well provided for, if we had but known how
    to be satisfied' (339). Burney's comedy *A Busy Day* ridicules both
    middle-class vulgarity and unthinking disdain for the middle
    class on the part of worthless aristocrats.
12. Straub finds irreconcilable contradictions in *Evelina*, but I see no
    contradiction between the idyllic romantic marriage of Evelina
    and Orville and the uncongenial one of the Mirvans, even if that
    may be closer to the norm; obviously, marriage, like most institu-
    tions, can be happy or unhappy depending on the circumstances.
13. See below, pp. 67–8.

Notes

14. Straub draws attention to this quotation, but interprets it a little differently (172–3).
15. Terry Castle reads the masquerade scene as 'an image of that paradisal realm of power and self-gratification out of which the Heiress (and her female creator) can only fall . . . a paradigmatic moment of wish-fulfillment' (270). In accordance with this reading, she sees the Harrels' disorderly household as more congenial than the Delviles', despite Burney's statements to the contrary. The masquerade and the Harrels' house represent a zone of freedom, which is succeeded by progressive loss and constriction (284) up to the depressing diminution of the heroine at the end.
16. The parallel with nakedness-dreams that Castle invokes reinforces this point, since the obvious implication of nakedness is exposure, deprivation of protective concealment. Regardless of the psychoanalytic interpretation of such dreams (Castle 272), the feeling they produce is painful embarrassment. Being looked at by everyone was not a pleasurable experience in Burney's view or that of eighteenth-century ladies in general.
17. Cf. Lady Mary Wortley Montagu, who insisted to her future husband that her feeling for him was friendship rather than 'love' 'because in the general sense that word is spoke, it signifies a passion rather founded on fancy than reason' (letter to Edward Wortley Montagu, 24 March 1711).
18. Regardless of the practical situation, the loss of her fortune would have diminished her status in eighteenth-century eyes; the money a woman brought into a marriage gave her status, even though her husband legally controlled it: George Farquhar's Mrs Sullen, for example, argues that her husband should treat her better because she brought him ten thousand pounds (*The Beaux' Stratagem* 2:1).
19. Cecilia's guilt at agreeing secretly to marry Delvile parallels Clarissa's for running away with Lovelace, and his arguments for marrying her to preserve or reclaim her reputation after the aborted secret marriage parallel those used to persuade Clarissa to marry Lovelace after the rape.

    Doody argues that Cecilia's mad scene does fit into the comic narrative, because it simply carries a little further the frustration that has plagued her in earlier scenes ('Deserts, Ruins . . .' 546–8).
20. When Burney entered society after the success of *Evelina*, she met George Owen Cambridge, a delightfully congenial young clergyman. She soon developed a serious interest in him, as, it seemed,

he did in her. Their social circle began to comment on his particularity. Yet months went by, and years, and it never seemed to occur to him that Burney probably would have liked to marry – she was now well into her thirties – and that he was the obvious candidate. Evidently he found her a pleasant and entertaining companion and had no compunctions about using her as such. Burney tortured herself trying to understand why he seemed to love but did not propose, to interpret the degree of his attachment from his slightest words and glances. Occasionally she gave way to anger: 'Who . . . could pardon except on a Death Bed . . . such wanton, such accumulating – such endless deceit & treachery? . . . his conduct has long past all mere impeachment of *trifling*, – it has seemed irrepressibly attached to me, – it has been deemed honourably serious by all our mutual acquaintances' (qtd Hemlow 192). She finally had to recognize that, despite his high principles, he was too cold and selfish to marry imprudently. When he did at last commit himself, it was to a beautiful and much younger woman.

During her painful suspense about Cambridge's attentions, Burney prided herself on absolute passivity. She wrote to Susanna in April 1783: 'I thank Heaven . . . that this is an affair in which I have been merely passive, however deeply concerned. What abundant reproach should I make myself for my own folly, and might the World make me for my own vanity, had I brought it on myself!' She 'has *no views* whatsoever, but . . . waits quietly till his own are devellop'd, before she will even ask *herself* what she *wishes* they should be' (qtd Doody, *Burney* 153). Doody uses this as evidence that Burney discovered that such passivity did not work, and therefore could not have endorsed Mr Tyrold's advice in *Camilla*.

One of Burney's few consolations at Court was her friendship with Colonel Stephen Digby, another attendant on the Queen. She found in him 'the most scrupulous good breeding,' 'the most acute sensibility,' 'soft and seducing manners,' and 'the tenderest social affections,' as well as the highest character (qtd Hemlow 205). He used to seek her out in her sitting room, where they had long sentimental conversations and read poetry to each other. All the while, she later found out, he was courting Miss Charlotte Gunning, a younger, prettier and richer woman. Obviously Digby, who seemed the most sensitive and high-principled of men, had seen nothing wrong with enlisting Burney's tender sympathy without making her any return. All she could do was exclaim indignantly that he was 'a man of double-dealing, & selfish artifice'; 'He has risked my whole Earthly peace, with a defiance of all mental integrity the most extraordinary to be imagined! He has committed a breach of all moral ties, with every semblance of every virtue!' (qtd Hemlow 212).

The circumstances, as opposed to the emotions, of the Camilla–Edgar relationship were drawn in part from Burney's experience with Jeremiah Crutchley, an eligible young man she met at the Thrales' house. The two liked and respected each other, but neither appreciated someone's remark that they should make a match. Although Burney herself was not pleased by this gossip, she was indignant to discover that Crutchley was filled with alarm and chagrin: 'these rich men think themselves the constant prey of all portionless girls, and are always upon their guard, and suspicious of some desire to take them in. . . . I determined to see as little of this most fearful and haughty gentleman in future as was in my power, since no good qualities can compensate for such arrogance of suspicion' (*DL* 1:478). Resentment at the selfishness of Cambridge, Digby and Crutchley lies behind Burney's presentation of Edgar; but she almost entirely defused it in characterizing him. Only in her last novel did she expose, in Sir Jaspar Herrington, the empty old age of a rich man who had carefully preserved himself from designing women by searching for flaws in any one who wanted to marry him.

21. Esther Burney wrote: 'Lionel is cruelly natural I fear' (qtd Hemlow 255).
22. Like W. S. Gilbert's Robin Oakapple, he 'combines the manners of a Marquis with the morals of a Methodist' (*Ruddigore* Act One).
23. Cf. Burney's affectionate reference to her 'ever unsuspicious Father' when she received a note from d'Arblay while their relationship was still secret: how fortunate no one else was present, she wrote to Susanna: 'My dear guileless Father alone could so soon have been satisfied [by her explanation], my extreme emotion considered, which made me stammer every word' (*JL* 2:48). Dr Burney also shared Mr Tyrold's concern for the world's opinion and would probably have given the same advice as that of his sermon-letter, in a similar situation.
24. The only exception, pointed out by Doody, is when she complains to Lavinia that he leads her on by his looks and manner, but thinks himself free because he has not actually proposed

(*Burney* 251–2). This of course was Burney's grievance against the two men who had hurt her, although it is not the worst of Edgar's faults.

25. The episode also makes the point that, although theoretically the duel over a woman's honor was a testimony of male devotion and chivalry, it was actually a parade of virility in which the contestants neither knew nor cared that they were embarrassing the woman they were supposed to be defending.

26. Burney's report of a conversation at Court among Mr Turbulent, Miss Planta and herself suggests that she endorsed the Tyrold–Gregory view of female education. Mr Turbulent argues that girls' education teaches them 'nothing but disguise, double-dealing, and falsehood'; Miss Planta calls this 'decorum and propriety'; Burney judges that Miss Planta was right 'in all essential points,' although Mr Turbulent argued better (*SL* 2:334).

27. Doody interprets Camilla's nightmare as a reflection of 'Burney's deepest fears and frustrations about being a writer, about having a right to speak, or being able to make any impression' (*Burney* 270). However, feelings appropriate to Burney are not so to artless Camilla. I find Doody's interpretation in 'Deserts, Ruins and Troubled Waters' more plausible: the pen that will not write signifies an 'impotent consciousness which tries to communicate its worth and is condemned ever to fail,' and thus the nightmare crystallizes the long frustration of Camilla's life (550–1).

28. Burney recognized that 'the World' would blame her for her marriage, but in her own case she justified herself by asserting d'Arblay's personal worth (*JL* 2:50).

29. That Burney intended Lady Honoria to be intelligent is indicated by a journal entry: 'Lady Warren . . . is giddy, gay, chatty, good-humoured, and a little affected; she hazards all that occurs to her, seems to think the world at her feet, and is so young, and gay, and handsome, that she is not much mistaken. She is, in short, an inferior Lady Honoria Pemberton: somewhat beneath her in parts and understanding . . .' (*DL* 2:109–10).

30. Burney's sister Esther and her family saw a similarity between Arlbery and Arblay, and Esther wrote: 'she has so much wit & sense that it is impossible not to like & almost love her' (qtd Doody, *Burney* 250).

31. The Admiral's combination of chivalry and antifeminism was probably drawn from a retired general described in Burney's journal, who is equally outraged by cruelty to 'fair females' (and other

helpless animals) and by the presumptuousness of a 'fair female' who studies Greek (*DL* 1:305–7). Nevertheless, the Admiral can rationalize away his chivalry when it suits him. Late in the book, he tells, without a blush, how he treated the woman he had promised to marry. On returning after some years in the East Indies, he blurted out his disappointment at how she had aged. He then used her request for some recompense for having waited so long for him as an excuse to walk out on his engagement.

32. Juliet can be more mature because her father figure, the wise Bishop, is off-stage during almost all of *The Wanderer*. However, she venerates him in true Burneyan fashion and would gladly sacrifice her happiness for his sake. She married her dreadful husband to save his life and is prepared to throw away the prospect of happy life in England by returning to her husband in France to protect the Bishop.

33. On the occasion of the Court's excursion to Oxford, the Queen unexpectedly entered the room where her exhausted attendants were sitting and eating. Burney was the only member of the group not to be embarrassed: 'I really think it quite respect sufficient never to sit down in the royal presence, without aiming at having it supposed I have stood bolt upright ever since I have been admitted to it.' She was also sufficiently emancipated to remark on the royal family's entrapment in their own etiquette, as she sympathized with the Queen and princesses for not being able to indulge their natural taste for conversation: 'They none of them do justice to their own minds, while they enforce this subjection upon the minds of others' (*DL* 2:475; 5:79).

34. Most of the men in the book are weakly sexed. Even the hero is excessively decorous and insufficiently forceful; and three major characters – young Ireton, Sir Jaspar Harrington and the Admiral – have backed away from marriage (Doody, *Burney* 344–6). Perhaps Burney is highlighting the absurdity of the convention that makes women dependent on men's strength.

35. The economic struggles of Wollstonecraft's Jemima are vividly rendered, but she is a secondary character in *The Wrongs of Woman* and not, of course, a lady. Inchbald's Agnes Primrose in *Nature and Art*, a peasant turned servant and prostitute, is realistically imagined; but she figures in a philosophical fiction and is not fully developed as a character. The emphasis in Hays's *The Victim of Prejudice* is more on the heroine's persecution by a fiendish baronet than on her difficulties in making her living.

36. Doody calls attention to Juliet's desolate vision of human existence shortly before the happy ending of *The Wanderer*: 'who can examine and meditate upon the uncertain existence of thy creatures – see failure without fault; success without virtue; sickness without relief; oppression in the very face of liberty; labour without sustenance; and suffering without crime; – and not see, and not feel that all call aloud for resurrection and retribution! that annihilation and justice would be one!' (*Burney* 367).

37. Belfield's self-indulgence is compounded by the unfair privilege given to men. Automatically favored over his sisters, he received an expensive education above his station, which he proceeded to squander. Never forced to stick to any course, he flits from one career to another, soon finding each one unbearably irksome. His complaint that writing to order was intolerable (883) simultaneously expresses Burney's own problems with forcing her gift and indicates how contemptibly self-indulgent he is: she herself often wrote when it was very difficult for her. Too proud to accept money from his wealthy friends, he obliviously lets his mother and sister sustain his life of luxury by depriving themselves. While his unregarded sister Henrietta does her duty whether she is unhappy or not, Belfield courts death when life does not meet his expectations. Although Burney presents noble aspiration and idealism in Belfield, she strongly emphasizes his vanity, selfishness and self-indulgence.

38. Harleigh's opinion echoes Burney's own, expressed in a letter to her father in 1792: she deplores 'French experiment upon the minds, manners, & powers of men, & the feasibility of expunging all past experience, for the purpose of treating the World as if it were created yesterday, & every man, woman, and Child, were let loose to act from their immediate suggestion, without reference to what is past, or simpathy in any thing that is present, or precaution for whatever is to come' (*JL* 1:230). Elinor's speech on p. 9 illustrates this French error.

39. As Doody has pointed out, Burney was unusually preoccupied with suicide. Perhaps she sensed a temptation in herself: like her own Camilla (and Austen's Marianne and Richardson's Clarissa), she reacted to intense emotional distress by wishing to die. When life at Court became intolerable for her, she developed an illness that she believed would end fatally.

40. Worthless young Ireton recognizes her love-slavery and longs for such a tribute himself (Doody, *Burney* 345).

41. Doody astutely notes that *The Wanderer* has the stock elements of a right-wing novel of the period – a guillotine scene (described), a vulgar male revolutionary sexually threatening an innocent female, and a mistaken petticoat radical – *and* those of a left-wing novel – a brutal husband exerting his legal rights, an aristocratic seducer of a lower-class innocent, poor working women, and respectable middle-class persons with crassly stupid anti-revolutionary attitudes (*Burney* 325).
42. See for instance *DL* 1:251.
43. Tompkins forcefully illustrated this double standard by quoting a critic in the *Critical Review* who, tiring of perfect heroes, longed for a new Tom Jones or Evelina – as if the faults of the two characters were equivalent (168).
44. Ann Radcliffe was another woman who took pains to develop the concept of female courage. See *The Italian* (1797) for an example of the heroine's courage in action (67–8) and *The Mysteries of Udolpho* (1794) for a disparagement of the stereotypically male courage that contrasts with it (358).
45. The woman novelist who portrayed true self-dependency was Sarah Scott, who drew in *A Description of Millennium Hall* (1762) a utopia of women who had got rid of men.
46. Burney reported that Lady De Ferrars told her that her husband, a Compton, 'always said that old Delvile was in the right not to give up the family name.' 'Is not this triumph for me, my dearest Susy? Pray let my daddy Crisp hear it, and knock under' (*DL* 2:125).

Works Cited

D'Arblay, Frances Burney, *A Busy Day*, ed. Tara Ghoshal Wallace (New Brunswick: Rutgers University Press, 1984).

D'Arblay, Frances Burney, *Camilla, or A Picture of Youth* (1796), ed. with an introd. by Edward A. and Lillian D. Bloom (Oxford: OUP, 1983).

D'Arblay, Frances Burney, *Cecilia, or Memoirs of an Heiress* (1782), ed. Peter Sabor and Margaret Anne Doody, with an introd. by Margaret Anne Doody (Oxford: OUP, 1988).

D'Arblay, Frances Burney, *The Diary and Letters of Madame d'Arblay*, ed. Charlotte Barrett with preface and notes by Austin Dobson (London: Macmillan and Co., 1904. 6 vols.).

D'Arblay, Frances Burney, *The Early Diary of Frances Burney 1768–1778*, ed. Annie Raine Ellis (London: George Bell, 1913. 2 vols.).

D'Arblay, Frances Burney, *Edwy and Elgiva*, ed. Miriam J. Benkovitz (Hamden, Conn.: Shoe String Press, 1957).

D'Arblay, Frances Burney, *Evelina, or The History of a Young Lady's Entrance into the World*, ed. with an introd. by Edward A. Bloom (London: OUP, 1968).

D'Arblay, Frances Burney, *The Journals and Letters of Fanny Burney (Madame d'Arblay)*, ed. Joyce Hemlow *et al.* (Oxford: Clarendon Press, 1972–84. 12 vols.).

D'Arblay, Frances Burney, 'Love and Fashion.' Manuscript in Berg Collection, New York Public Library.

D'Arblay, Frances Burney, *Memoirs of Dr. Charles Burney* (London: Edward Moxon, 1932; rpt. New York: AMS, 1975. 3 vols.).

D'Arblay, Frances Burney, *The Wanderer, or Female Difficulties* (1814). Introd. by Margaret Drabble (London: Pandora Press, 1988).

D'Arblay, Frances Burney, 'The Witlings. A Comedy.' Manuscript in Berg Collection, New York Public Library.

D'Arblay, Frances Burney, 'The Woman Hater. A Comedy in Five Acts.' Manuscript in Berg Collection, New York Public Library.

Works cited

Austen, Jane, *Jane Austen's Letters to Her sister Cassandra and Others*, ed. R. W. Chapman (Oxford: Clarendon Press, 1932).

Austen, Jane, *Pride and Prejudice* (1813) (New York: New American Library, 1961).

Austen, Jane, *Sense and Sensibility* (1811) (New York: New American Library, 1961).

Barbauld, Anna Laetitia, ed., *The British Novelists; with an Essay; and Prefaces, Biographical and Critical* (London: F.C. and J. Rivington *et al.*, 1810. 50 vols.).

Bloom, Lillian D. and Edward A., 'Fanny Burney's Novels: The Retreat from Wonder,' *Novel* 12 (1979), 215–35.

Boswell, James, Life of Johnson (London, Oxford University Press, 1953).

Brissenden, R. F., *Virtue in Distress: Studies in the Novel of Sentiment from Richardson to Sade* (New York: Barnes and Noble, 1974).

Brooke, Frances, *The Excursion* (1779) (London: T. Cadell, 1785. 2 vols.).

Burke, Edmund, *Reflections on the Revolution in France* (1790) (New York: Rinehart, 1959).

Burney, Charles, *Memoirs of Dr. Charles Burney 1726–1769*, ed. Slava Klima, Garry Bowers and Kerry S. Grant (Lincoln: University of Nebraska Press, 1988).

Castle, Terry, *Masquerade and Civilization: The Carnivalesque in Eighteenth Century English Culture and Fiction* (Stanford: Stanford University Press, 1986).

Chapone, Hester Mulso, *The Works of Mrs. Chapone* (Boston: W. Wells and T. B. Wait, 1809. 4 vols. in 2).

Cohn, Jan, *Romance and the Erotics of Property: Mass-Market Fiction for Women* (Durham: Duke University Press, 1988).

Critical Review, reviews of *Cecilia*, December 1782, pp. 414–20; of *Camilla*, September 1796, pp. 26–40; of *The Wanderer*, April 1814, pp. 405–24.

Cutting, Rose Marie, 'Defiant Women: The Growth of Feminism in Fanny Burney's Novels,' *SEL* 17 (1977), 519–30.

Cutting, Rose Marie, 'A Wreath for Fanny Burney's Last Novel: *The Wanderer*'s Contribution to Women's Studies,' *CLA Journal* 20 (1976), 57–67.

Delany, Mary, *The Autobiography and Correspondence of Mrs. Delany*, ed. Sarah Chauncey Woolsey (Boston: Roberts Brothers, 1879. 2 vols.).

Devlin, D. D., *The Novels and Journals of Fanny Burney* (New York: St Martin's Press, 1987).

Works cited

Doody, Margaret Anne, 'Deserts, Ruins and Troubled Waters: Female Dreams in Fiction and the Development of the Gothic Novel,' GENRE 10 (1977), 529–72.

Doody, Margaret Anne, *Frances Burney: The Life in the Works* (New Brunswick: Rutgers University Press, 1988).

Edgeworth, Maria, *Letters for Literary Ladies* (1795) (New York: Garland, 1974).

Edgeworth, Maria and Richard, *Practical Education* (1798) (New York: Garland, 1974. 2 vols.).

Edinburgh Review, review of *The Wanderer*, April 1815, pp. 336–8.

Epstein, Julia, *The Iron Pen: Frances Burney and the Politics of Women's Writing* (Madison: University of Wisconsin Press, 1989).

Fergus, Jan, *Jane Austen and the Didactic Novel* (Totowa, NJ: Barnes and Noble, 1983).

Gilman, Charlotte Perkins, 'The Yellow Wallpaper' in *The Norton Anthology of Literature by Women*, ed. Sandra Gilbert and Susan Gubar (New York: Norton, 1985).

Gisborne, Thomas, *An Enquiry into the Duties of the Female Sex* (1797) (New York: Garland, 1974).

Gregory, Dr John, *A Father's Legacy to His Daughters* (1774) (New York: Garland, 1974).

Griffith, Elizabeth and Richard, *A Series of Genuine Letters between Henry and Frances* (London: W. Johnston, 1767. 3rd edn. 6 vols.).

Hamilton, Elizabeth, *Memoirs of Modern Philosophers* (1800) (New York: Garland, 1974. 3 vols.).

Hays, Mary, *Appeal to the Men of Great Britain in Behalf of Women* (1798) (New York: Garland, 1974).

Hays, Mary, *Memoirs of Emma Courtney* (1796) (New York: Hugh M. Griffith, 1802. 2 vols. in 1).

Haywood, Eliza, *The History of Miss Betsy Thoughtless* (London: T. Gardner, 1751. 4 vols.).

Hemlow, Joyce, *The History of Fanny Burney* (Oxford: Clarendon Press, 1958).

Inchbald, Elizabeth, *A Simple Story* (1791), ed. J. M. S. Tompkins (London: OUP, 1967).

Johnson, Claudia L., *Jane Austen: Women, Politics, and the Novel* (Chicago: University of Chicago Press, 1988).

Johnson, R. Brimley, ed., *Fanny Burney and the Burneys* (New York: Frederick A. Stokes Co., 1926).

Johnson, Samuel, *The Selected Writings of Samuel Johnson*, ed. Katharine Rogers (New York: New American Library, 1981).

Works cited

Kolodny, Annette, 'The Integrity of Memory: Creating a New Literary History of the United States,' *American Literature* 57 (May 1985), 292–307.

Lennox, Charlotte, *Euphemia* (London: T. Cadell and J. Evans, 1790. 4 vols.).

Lennox, Charlotte, *The Female Quixote* (1752), ed. Margaret Dalziel (London: OUP, 1970).

Montagu, Lady Mary Wortley, *The Complete Letters*, ed. Robert Halsband (Oxford: Clarendon Press, 1965. 3 vols.).

Monthly Review, reviews of *Cecilia*, December 1782, pp. 453–7, of *Camilla*, October 1796, pp. 156–63, of *The Wanderer*, April 1815, pp. 413–15.

More, Hannah, *Strictures on the Modern System of Female Education* (1799) (New York: Garland, 1974. 2 vols.).

More, Hannah, *Coelebs in Search of a Wife* (1809) (New York: Derby and Jackson, 1857).

Piozzi, Hester Lynch Thrale, *Thraliana: The Diary of Mrs. Hester Lynch Thrale (Later Mrs. Piozzi) 1776–1809*, ed. Katharine C. Balderston (Oxford: Clarendon Press, 1942, 2 vols.).

Polwhele, Richard, *The Unsex'd Females* (London: T. Cadell and W. Davies, 1798).

Radcliffe, Ann, *The Italian* (1797), ed. Frederick Garber (London: OUP, 1971).

Radcliffe, Ann, *The Mysteries of Udolpho* (1794), ed. Bonamy Dobrée (London: OUP, 1970).

Radcliffe, Mary Ann, *The Female Advocate* (1799) (New York: Garland, 1974).

Richardson, Samuel, *Clarissa, or The History of a Young Lady* (1747–8) (Oxford: Basil Blackwell, 1930. 8 vols.).

Richardson, Samuel, *The History of Sir Charles Grandison* (1753–4) (Oxford: Basil Blackwell, 1930. 6 vols.).

Scott, Sarah, *A Description of Millennium Hall* (1762) (New York: Bookman Associates, 1955).

Simons, Judy, *Fanny Burney* (Totowa, NJ: Barnes and Noble, 1987).

Smith, Charlotte, *The Banished Man* (London: T. Cadell and W. Davies, 1794. 4 vols.).

Smith, Charlotte, *Desmond* (London: G. G. J. and J. Robinson, 1792. 3 vols.).

Smith, Charlotte, *Emmeline: The Orphan of the Castle* (1788), ed. Anne Henry Ehrenpreis (London: OUP, 1971).

Smith, Charlotte, *Marchmont* (London: Sampson Low, 1796. 4 vols.).

Works cited

Smith, Charlotte, *The Old Manor House* (1793), ed. Anne Henry Ehrenpreis (London: OUP, 1969).

Smith, Charlotte, *The Young Philosopher* (London: T. Cadell, 1798. 4 vols.).

Spacks, Patricia M., 'Ev'ry Woman Is at Heart a Rake,' *Eighteenth-Century Studies*, 8 (1974), 27–46.

Spacks, Patricia M., *Imagining a Self: Autobiography and Novel in Eighteenth Century England* (Cambridge, Mass.: Harvard University Press, 1976).

Staves, Susan, '*Evelina*; or, Female Difficulties,' *Modern Philology* 73 (1976), 368–81.

Straub, Kristina, *Divided Fictions: Fanny Burney and Feminine Strategy* (Lexington: University Press of Kentucky, 1987).

Todd, Janet, *Sensibility: An Introduction* (London: Methuen, 1986).

Tompkins, J. M. S., *The Polite Marriage* (Cambridge: CUP, 1938).

Tompkins, J. M. S., *The Popular Novel in England 1770–1800* (1932) (Lincoln: University of Nebraska Press, 1971).

Wakefield, Priscilla, *Reflections on the Present Condition of the Female Sex* 1978 (New York: Garland, 1974).

Wollstonecraft Godwin, Mary, *Posthumous Works of the Author of A Vindication of the Rights of Woman*, with 'Memoirs' by William Godwin (1798) (Clifton: Augustus M. Kelley, 1972. 4 vols. in 2).

Wollstonecraft, Mary, *A Vindication of the Rights of Woman* (1792), ed. Miriam Brady Kramnick (Harmondsworth: Penguin, 1975).

Index

Index

Index

Index

Index